Simon & Schuster's

GUIDE TO
Bonsai

Gianfranco Giorgi

Photography by Enzo Arnone

Edited by Victoria Jahn,
Brooklyn Botanic Garden

A FIRESIDE BOOK
PUBLISHED BY SIMON & SCHUSTER INC.

ACKNOWLEDGMENTS

The Publisher wishes to thank the following for their kind assistance: Prof. Maria Francesca Morea, Prof. Mara Giuliattini, Dr. Francesco Birardi
For help with the illustrations: Mauro Bini, Florence; Francesco Birardi, Florence; Danilo Bonacchi, Pistoia; Elio Boni, Florence; Guido Degl'Innocenti, Tavarnuzze (Florence); Andrea Niccolai, Lucca; Günther Ruhe, Cassano Spinola (Alessandria); Mario Starace, Triest; Luciano Viaro, Triest; Nicola Zannotti, Florence
Special thanks to: Bonsai Centrum, Heidelberg; Centro Bonsai Franchi, Ponte all'Abate, Pescia (Pistoia)

F

FIRESIDE
Simon & Schuster Building
Rockefeller Center
1230 Avenue of the Americas
New York, New York 10020

© 1990 Arnoldo Mondadori Editore S.p.A., Milan
© 1990 in the English translation Arnoldo Mondadori Editore S.p.A., Milan

English translation by John Gilbert

Art Director: Giorgio Seppi
Symbols by Simona Aguzzoni
Introduction illustrations by Vittorio Salarolo
Botanical Table illustrations by Lino Simeoni

First published in Italian in 1990
by Arnoldo Mondadori Editore S.p.A.
under the title *Bonsai*
Typeset by Rowland Phototypesetting Ltd, Bury St Edmunds, Suffolk, England

Printed and bound in Spain by Artes Gráficas Toledo, S.A.
D.L.TO: 310-1997

10 9 8 7

Library of Congress Cataloging in Publication Data
Giorgi, Gianfranco.
    (Tutto bonsai, English)
    Simon & Schuster's guide to bonsai/by Gianfranco Giorgi:
  edited by Victoria Jahn.
        p.   cm.
  "A Fireside book."
    Translation of: Tutto bonsai.
    Includes bibliographical references.
    ISBN 0-671-73488-1
    1. Bonsai.   I Jahn, Victoria. 1948–.   II. Title.   III. Title:
  Simon and Schuster's guide to bonsai.
  IV. Title: Guide to bonsai. V. Title: Bonsai.
  SB433.5.G56 1990
  635.9'772—dc20   90-20778
                                                         CIP

CONTENTS

NOTE

The bonsai are listed under their botanical
names. The common name, if there is one, can
be found in the MEASUREMENTS AND
SOURCES section on pages 243–246.

KEY TO SYMBOLS

indoor or
outdoor tree

indoor tree

outdoor tree

water
sparingly

water
normally

water
generously

site in
shade

site in
semi-shade

site in
full sun

quite easy
to grow

easy to
grow

difficult
to grow

Although the growing of bonsai is no longer looked upon nowadays as an odd or eccentric activity, there is still a good deal of mystery attached to the term and its deeper meaning. More and more people visit shows in which dwarf trees are exhibited and although the questions they ask and the explanations they seek are sometimes naive, their interest is genuine.

Bonsai is the final result of a variety of disciplines – horticultural, technical, artistic, and philosophical – all so closely connected that the absence of any one of them can cause the whole process to fall short of the perfection which is the aim of every true enthusiast. Each plant has its specific needs, often varying from one climatic zone to another and must be tended individually using specialized techniques. Apart from these, the grower must have the eye of an artist and must display a love and respect for the plant very akin to the philosophical notions of the Orient. There, a tree is not only seen for what it is but also envisaged as something born of the earth and approaching heaven – not simply an object, but a piece of the universe, with its own life and its own spirit.

The links which exist between the grower of bonsai and his tree are uncommonly deep, not to be found in any other branch of gardening. Most of us love flowers for their beauty and gaiety, and many of us derive powerful sensations of tranquillity, strength, and protection from trees and forests. Creating a bonsai, however, is not just a matter

of raising a plant in a pot but of cultivating the very spirit of this plant. It is not merely an attempt to simulate the form of the fully grown tree but rather to establish a caring, everyday relationship with the plant and with the natural phenomena – wind, rain, frost, and drought – which mold it. In this way, we are brought closer to nature.

Bonsai is today quite fashionable but the tendency is perhaps to give more consideration to the object itself than to its creation, forgetting that bonsai expresses itself through living material and that in time it can be changed and transformed. Strictly speaking, there are no truly finished bonsai but only plants at different stages of cultivation. The real bonsai enthusiast seeks not only enjoyment but also enrichment of experience. In contrast to other forms of art, the pleasure comes not so much from completing the work as from the act of creating it.

The word "art" is deliberately chosen here. None of us who practice bonsai consciously regard ourselves as artists, but in the case of many time-honored masterpieces in private and public collections, this goal has been achieved. Rather than bonsai, they can justifiably be called "living sculptures."

In this book I have endeavored to summarize some of my experiences in the ranks of bonsai enthusiasts. I have had the rare opportunity of seeing some of the world's greatest bonsai masterpieces and the pleasure of working with the most famous practitioners as well as

In this painting by Maruyama Okyo (eighteenth cent.) several elements common to Oriental art and to bonsai may be observed: simplicity, naturalness, essentiality and distribution of spaces. A Kaki branch is at the same time a fragment, and a unique and finished whole which creates a poetic image of reality as conveyed by the artist's sensibility.

with others perhaps less celebrated but equally important. To them I owe all my knowledge and I offer them my thanks. I would like to add that their teachings have not only afforded me the chance to understand bonsai but also to appreciate two fundamental truths.

The first is the lesson of humility. No one is omniscient, yet each of us, through our work and experience, can claim to have made a modest contribution to the understanding of nature's grand scheme. The second is the awareness that in spite of individual differences, there are fundamental values that are the common legacy of every civilization.

This book, with its wealth of illustrations, aims to be a true dictionary of bonsai, in which 140 species are described, with general information from various sources and practical suggestions on cultivation procedures.

My hope is that the book will help to popularize an art which does not depend for its success on mysterious secrets of alchemy but simply on the knowledge of techniques that are sometimes quite elementary and, above all, on constant attention and love.

THE PHILOSOPHY OF BONSAI

An attempt to explain the background of bonsai entails clarifying a situation which even authorities in the Orient tend to present in different ways. Since it is important to provide Western readers with a general survey of the subject which they can understand and find useful, there is no point, in my opinion, in delving too deeply into a philosophical-religious debate as complex as that of the Japanese. It would be like trying to evaluate the universe with a tape measure.

Nevertheless, if we wish to understand bonsai in some depth we must endeavor to grasp certain facts which go far beyond the surface. In the first place we have to realize that bonsai developed primarily in Japan, where certain aesthetic, philosophical, and religious values already existed: a taste for refinement based on simplicity; Shinto (a religion, a philosophy, and a national belief), the deepest essence of which is founded on communion with nature; and the doctrine of Zen, which introduced *Wabi* and *Sabi*, fundamental concepts which, with *Kami*, form the triad inspiring the art of bonsai.

Kami – synonymous with "divinity" – may be defined, where bonsai is concerned, as the spirit or interior force of things, human artefacts, natural events and, of course, plants, inasmuch as these can be sources of almost religious inspiration.

Wabi can be related, for us in the West, to the Franciscan conception of life, in the sense of inner harmony, well-being, and gratification, which we can experience by meditating on the grandeur of natural manifestations. *Wabi* conveys the notion of humility when confronted by nature, of acceptance of natural events. Such a concept does not place man in the center of the universe but rather as part of a universal design which is completely in balance with itself.

Sabi, on the other hand, is the pleasure in possessing, tending, and loving things which have been transformed by man, nature, and the passage of time. *Sabi* is also characterized by the possession of simplicity, austerity, and venerability.

A fundamental and illuminating insight into the world of bonsai is provided by an article written by Kyuzo Murata, a leading authority from Omiya, who for many years curated the Emperor of Japan's bonsai collection. In the article, reproduced here on pp. 15–18, Murata gives a clear explanation of the sentiments of *Wabi* and *Sabi* in relation to bonsai but admits that they are in practice accessible only to the Japanese. I do not entirely agree with this statement.

I believe, rather, that these feelings are to some extent universally valid and that every practitioner of bonsai is – no matter how vaguely – aware of them. Moreover I maintain that if a method of loving and caring for plants has managed to make such giant strides in a world where consumerism is so widely accepted as a model for living, there has to be a good reason for it. May it not be a form of protest against an everyday relationship between ourselves and nature which has become increasingly remote and contrived?

In a world which is always in a hurry, the cultivation of bonsai may teach us that impatience often leads to failure, and that natural phenomena such as drought, rain, snow, and frost are still part and parcel of our lives and may prevent us from carrying out our plans. Tending a tree, understanding its mechanisms and its needs may also make us realize that our very survival depends on plants. The creation of a bonsai is a constant and wonderful reminder that nature is not the servant of man.

HISTORY

Bonsai was born in the Orient, most probably in China. The rare and fragmentary historical documents on the subject have been variously interpreted, and there has been a widespread tendency, which continues to this day and is not wholly unrelated to commercial interests, to seek and appropriate its ancient origins and noble antecedents.

Among the countless legends that are told, it is worth recalling one simple explanation which traces the origins of bonsai to plants raised in pots for medicinal purposes.

Plants have always played an important role in Chinese medicine, so it is easy to imagine that sooner or later someone would decide to grow plants in pots rather than go out to look for them. Such plants, continuously trimmed would eventually have taken on such a pleasing appearance that they would begin to be raised for ornamental purposes. Perhaps this explains the origin of *Penzai*, the earliest known form of *Penjing* and of *Bonsai*.

If we accept the idea that bonsai is an art, we must appreciate that it has gradually changed and evolved over time. I am convinced that plants were originally kept in pots merely for the sake of a few

Kyuzo Murata is among the most respected and loved Japanese masters. His essay, inspired by sentiments rooted in tradition, philosophy, and religion, is, for Westerners, one of the most important texts for the understanding of bonsai.

It was around 1960 when people all over the world started to understand a word, bonsai. Of course, few enthusiasts knew the word until then, for mostly it was called dwarfed plant, potted tree, or miniature tree. In 1970 a huge-scale bonsai show was staged at the Osaka Expo. I believe Expo really played a major role in promoting the word bonsai to all foreign visitors.

Questions often arose at Expo and later. "What is the definition of bonsai? What is the difference between bonsai and Hachiuye, which means potted plant?" The answer is not simple. I usually give the following definition:

Bonsai is a living plant transferred to a pot or tray or a rock or stone so that it can continue to live semi-permanently. It has not only a natural beauty of the particular plant but the appearance reminds people of something other than the plant itself. It could be a scene, a forest or part of a forest, a lone tree in the field, a seascape, a lake, a river or a stream or a pond. It is also possible that a certain appearance reminds a person of the wind blowing through the branches.

In Japan, the meaning of bonsai is to create a natural scene on the tray, using plants as the main materials. When you take a Hachiuye, or potted plant, you can only see "prettiness of the plant or flower." It does not remind you of anything else. It is possible, however, to change the Hachiuye into bonsai by using what we call bonsai technique. By adapting the techniques of Yoseuye (group planting) and Ne Tsuranari (root connecting), we can make the scene look like a forest or part of a forest. Shaken or slanting style, will remind you of wind blowing; Kengai or cascade style, will remind you of a cliff.

The next question is "Can we add grasses or materials other than plants?" There are many people who believe the grasses or stones or rocks are an important decoration of bonsai. They help improve the appearance of bonsai. In a way I agree with them. I would not say that all kinds of grasses should be employed, but some are quite usable and sometimes they will make fine bonsai. There are certain kinds of grasses or stones that remind one of a grass field, or rocks in rapids or murmuring streams.

At the extreme limit I believe that even tulips or hyacinths can be used with bonsai. Back in the early 1950s I used to see many banana-tree bonsai about 10 inches high, but I do not see them now. In a way I feel sorry that I don't see them anymore in Japan.

The bonsai spirit

What I have discussed so far is a general conception in the Japanese bonsai world, and I am sure you are all familiar with the idea. Let us now proceed a little further, a little deeper. The art of bonsai was developed in Japan where there were four seasons, clear water, and clean air all over the country, a 1500-year-old history with many ancient but unchanging traditions or customs.

Among all these things the art of bonsai has grown to be what it is today.

I do not think that bonsai could have developed and survived in tropical or frozen zones or in the deserts. Bonsai's association with the change of seasons, mountains, valleys, rivers, waters, lakes, storms, gentle wind, rains, snow, frost, and many other natural phenomena is far more important than one can imagine. Japan is one of the few fortunate countries that have all of these.

Bonsai should not be a mere sketch of a scene, or a three-dimensional exhibit from a photograph of a scene.

It is perfectly all right to use nature as the subject, but the goal should be a sketch which has been refined and trimmed in your mind before you start creating. Only then you can call it an art.

For instance, in Japan, we have the traditional Noh play or classic Japanese dance, which is the product of three-dimensional music and story. In your country you have ballet. If ballet can be defined as a fusion or union of human sensibility and art, then bonsai can be defined as a union of nature and art.

The Noh play or ballet expresses its movement in a relatively short period of time; on the other hand, you can hardly notice the slow growth of bonsai. The object of bonsai is to simulate nature. Nature expresses eternity in very, very slow movement and bonsai demonstrates this concept of the slow process of nature. When your concept of bonsai comes this far, then you cannot avoid going into the world of Wabi or Sabi. It is an almost impossible task to try to explain the meaning of these terms because they are concepts of feeling which were created and actually only felt by Japanese people over many, many generations; they were unknown to Westerners until recently.

Wabi is a state of mind, or a place, or environment in tea ceremony, or in Haiku. It is a feeling of great simplicity, quiet yet dignified. Sabi is a feeling of simplicity and quietness which comes from something that is old and used over and over again. For an instant, picture yourself standing at a corner of Ryoanji's stone garden in Kyoto in the evening, in late autumn in a misty rain. You are viewing the garden; the next moment you close your eyes and are deep in thought. Actually there is nothing in your mind. It is empty, and yet your mind or heart is fulfilled with certain contentment. That feeling is Wabi.

I firmly believe the final goal of creating bonsai is to create this feeling of Wabi, or Sabi in bonsai. This is the ultimate goal of the art of bonsai. I do not have the knowledge to explain the essence of Wabi, or Sabi, but I cannot help but think that the essence of philosophy is to seek truth, virtue, and beauty, and it so happens that these are the essence of bonsai.

The feeling of Wabi, or Sabi, is something almost stoic which eventually leads us to Zen Buddhism. These are not easy-going feelings; they are very disciplined, quiet but severe. The feelings are common among people who are very religious and people who create bonsai. I think this feeling is love, love for trees, love for human beings.

No single technique

Now, let us go back to reality. Bonsai is a strange art wherein one can produce a feeling of the reality of nature by manipulation, over a long period of time, of trees, stones, rocks, trays or pots. And every bonsai is original. No two are alike. You can never finish or complete the creation of bonsai. It goes on and on forever.

In the art of bonsai, there is no particular school for teaching technique as you have in flower arrangement. This is because we must protect the life of a tree permanently. Limiting the bonsai technique to a certain style is to ignore the physiology of the tree. If you try to enforce your own particular design on the tree without considering its nature, the tree may eventually die. Plant physiology is limited. You need to understand this limitation as you create your bonsai.

Apart from trees in the field or forest, trees in bonsai trays or pots are, I believe, the longest living plants which you help to grow and sustain with love, and which share your joys and sorrows. They say the life span of an average cherry tree in nature is about 120 years, but it is not rare to see much older cherry trees as bonsai. It becomes a sort of religion when you start loving a bonsai which has a much longer life span than your own.

All of you who are actually engaged in the art of bonsai have at one time or another studied under fine bonsai teachers and have mastered the techniques of Chokkan or upright style, Moyogi or octopus style, Shakan or slanting style, and Kengai or cascade style, but when it comes to Nebari – arranging root systems or branches – you realize that it does not always work as it is taught.

I have been working with bonsai for the past 60 years, and I still come across problems almost every day – about fertilizing, about soil for planting, about watering, about stones or rocks, about wiring. There is no way to make a fast decision. One sometimes takes several years to arrive at a solution. So, recently I have come to my own conclusion that the most challenging technique in the art of bonsai is to transform a most unnatural-looking tree into a most natural-looking tree.

For instance, there was a famous zelkova which was owned by the late Prime Minister Shigura Yoshida, who happened to be Chairman of Nippon Bonsai Association at the time. This bonsai was created by Mr Ogata. He had severed the main trunk of the zelkova and created a totally new look. When I first saw it at the annual Kokufukai Exhibition, I laughed, and so did the directors of national museums who attended the exhibition. Several years later it was again exhibited at the Tokyo Olympics and people liked it this time. Some years later it was displayed at another Kokufukai Exhibition, and this time it was recognized as one of the finest bonsai in Japan. It really is a strange looking tree. You would never find such an unnatural-looking tree anywhere in the world, yet it looks exactly like a huge zelkova tree standing alone and strong in the field.

Let me deviate to another example. In a Japanese Kubuki play, a male actor plays the role of a female. We call him Oyama. The audience knows that she is he, but he really acts and looks like a woman. This is an art. The same thing can be said about the art of bonsai.

In Japan and China, we have what we call the art of handwriting, or calligraphy. There are three basic ways of writing Kanji, just as in the West there are two basic ways of writing alphabets, capital letters and small letters. I think we can apply the same variation to bonsai. When you try to sketch natural scenery, you may use either capital letters or small letters because the basic goal is the same, but your method of approaching this goal is different.

Fortunately, there is a replica of the Ryoanji Temple Stone Garden at Brooklyn Botanic Garden. For those who have not seen the garden, visit it if you have a chance. Just stand there and watch; if you are tired, close your eyes. I am sure this experience will help you to understand more about bonsai.

(Our grateful thanks to Elizabeth Scholtz, director of the Brooklyn Botanic Gardens, New York for granting permission to reproduce this article.)

The ancient wall painting found in the tomb of Prince Zhang Huai contains a question to which no answer has yet been given. Why does he wish to be accompanied on his last journey by two Penjing (bonsai)? Did he perhaps love them in his lifetime or are they merely a tribute to a person of power? It is clear, in any event, that Penjing were even then regarded as something important, beautiful and precious.

characteristic details – type of leaf, flowers, fruits or trunk structure – and that only as time passed did they assume the appearance of miniature trees; and I will go further to maintain that the elegance and the perfection to which we now aspire in the creation of bonsai is a conception that was brought to fruition only in the present century.

The oldest testimony to the presence of bonsai in China was discovered in Shaanxi province by archaeologists as recently as 1972, in the tomb of Prince Zhang Huai, of the Tang dynasty, who died 706 A.D. The paintings of two servants on the tomb wall show one carrying a miniature landscape with rocks and plants, and the other a pot in the form of a lotus flower containing a tree with green leaves and red fruits. It is interesting to note how this painting anticipates, to some extent, the bonsai creations of modern China. Penjing – as bonsai is called in that country – is in fact divided into two categories: "Shan Shui Penjing," a landscape with rocks, water, and sometimes plants, and "She Zhuang Penjing," a plant in a pot.

Many schools of bonsai flourish in China: Suzhou, Yanghzhou, Shanghai, and Sichuan. But it is the Lingnan school that is best known in the West, for it was the first to shape the plant solely through pruning – without relying on wires or other mechanical means. By alternating drastic pruning of the new branches with periods when the plant was left to grow freely, trees with dramatic forms were produced. Obviously this method was only practicable with those species that could withstand the traumas of the pruning process.

China influenced Japanese culture in many ways and certainly

bonsai reached Japan from that land. Brought by monks, merchants, and court officials, this art was well-established in Japan by the thirteenth century. For a long time the practice was reserved for the ruling feudal and religious classes. Techniques were gradually improved and both the plants and containers became more refined. Plants were progressively simplified, tending increasingly to imitate trees in nature (although in recent times there has been a pronounced tendency to go for more spectacular and dramatic effects). The containers, too, have evolved from the elaborate Chinese antiques favored in early times to the simple, elegantly shaped and delicately colored pots of today.

By the twentieth century, the Japanese had codified the various styles and classes and in 1935 bonsai was officially recognized as an art.

Some of the earliest bonsai in the West likewise came from Japan. Introduced during the Third Universal Exhibition in Paris (1878) and later displayed at the 1889 and 1900 exhibitions, the plants aroused much curiosity and were eventually sold at auction – fetching extraordinary prices for the time. A Thuja more than 200 years old, for example, sold for the astonishing figure of 1,300 francs.

At about the same time various bonsai were imported into England and displayed by the Japanese at the London Exhibition of 1909. Moreover, it is said that King Edward VII had a collection in which he took a keen personal interest.

Although all trace has been lost of these plants in Europe, the

Arnold Arboretum at Harvard University still has several specimens collected around 1913 by the U.S. Ambassador to Japan, Larz Anderson, and presented to the Arboretum in 1937. Brooklyn Botanic Garden likewise has a collection of Japanese bonsai dating from 1916. But despite these few examples, which aroused curiosity and interest, bonsai was not truly established in the West until after the Second World War. In the United States a number of Japanese immigrants found ready support among certain Americans, who as a result of wartime events had come into contact with this ancient civilization, and formed the first groups of enthusiasts. From North America interest spread to other English-speaking countries and then all over the world.

Paradoxically, the enormous fascination that this art has exerted on the West has stimulated a revival of bonsai in Japan itself, where it had been briefly eclipsed after the war as a result of its close links with a world of ancient traditions that had been engulfed by military events.

Today bonsai is a profitable business. However, those who actively practice it, for whom the term "bonsaist" has been coined, are for the most part amateurs and enthusiasts, and the renown which bonsai enjoys almost everywhere is in no small measure due to their creativity.

In recent years, apart from collections in China and Japan, the fame of bonsai has been disseminated by four principal collections open to the public: the U.S. National Bonsai Collection in Washington D.C., the Brooklyn Botanic Garden in New York, the Jardin Botanique de Montréal in Canada and the Bonsai Museum of Heidelberg in the

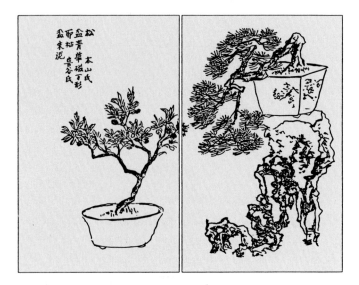

German Federal Republic. The Bonsai Museum of Heidelberg and the U.S. National Bonsai Collection merit special mention.

The former is the only important international collection in Europe. Planned and created by a shrewd businessman, it contains superb works by leading Japanese and American masters as well as a fine collection of antique pots.

The Washington collection, appropriately established inside the National Arboretum, owes its creation to a gesture of popular friendship and reconciliation, being a gift to the United States from Japan on the occasion of the 1976 Bicentenary. This donation was accorded special quarantine to accommodate the strict plant import regulations enforced by the United States. New pavilions, paid for entirely by bonsai enthusiasts, will soon be added to the original nucleus – one for American bonsai, the other for Chinese bonsai. Two specimens of Japanese bonsai were donated by King Hassan II of Morocco and, not by chance, the first American plant was offered by the great master John Yoshio Naka. This was the famous forest planting of junipers called "Go-shin" ("Guardian of the Spirit"). Recently a *Pinus ponderosa*, about 500 years old, was collected and worked on by the American master Dan Robinson and presented to the foundation on behalf of the U.S. Forest Service. An entire collection of Chinese bonsai was also donated by the master Wu Yee-Sun of Hong Kong.

Today there are more and more shows, competitions for beginners, and advanced practitioners, and national and international conventions arranged by companies and various associations. Apart from the obvious commercial interests involved, such initiatives foster friendships and ever closer relations among the world's bonsai enthusiasts. The idea, promoted by the Japanese and generally accepted, is, "to bring people closer to nature and one another through bonsai."

Not everything, of course, is as idyllic as it sounds, and bonsai enthusiasts themselves are under no illusion of being able to change international political relationships or even human relationships. But it is surely true that one small thing which unites, is better than a hundred others, far bigger, which divide.

THE PHYSIOLOGY OF THE TREE

From a physiological point of view a tree may be compared to an industrial complex, extracting the substances it needs from the ground and air and with the help of the sun's energy converting them in its "chemical laboratory" into the materials necessary for the life of the whole complex. This complex can be divided into three principal parts, each inseparable from the others, which nevertheless perform specific tasks: roots, trunk and branches, and leaves.

Roots
The roots constitute the subterranean part of the tree and perform four essential functions. They anchor the tree to the ground, absorb and transport water and minerals from the soil to the stem, and serve as food storage organs.

In most young trees, the tap-root or principal root is generally predominant. As the tree matures, finer roots extend like rays in the surface layer of the soil, beneath the tree's crown and several feet beyond. In the majority of species associated with bonsai the root system spreads laterally through the soil, forming an amazing network of progressively finer roots eventually terminating in the outermost zone of root hairs which, alone, are capable of absorbing minerals and water from the ground. The roots often live in symbiosis with fungus filaments (mycorrhizae). These surround and penetrate the roots and in this way increase the absorbing surface of the roots. They may make certain minerals available to the root from the soil which otherwise would be inaccessible. In return the fungus obtains energy from the food stored in the outer cells. A root without the proper mycorrhizal fungi in the soil will not grow well.

Trunk and branches
Continuing the industrial imagery, the trunk and branches of the tree perform many functions: flexible support of the leafy canopy or "chemical laboratory" as it reaches for the energy source (light); transport of minerals and water extracted by the roots to the leaves and redistribution of the food manufactured by the leaves to all parts of the tree. Trunk and branches are divided into the following principal sections:

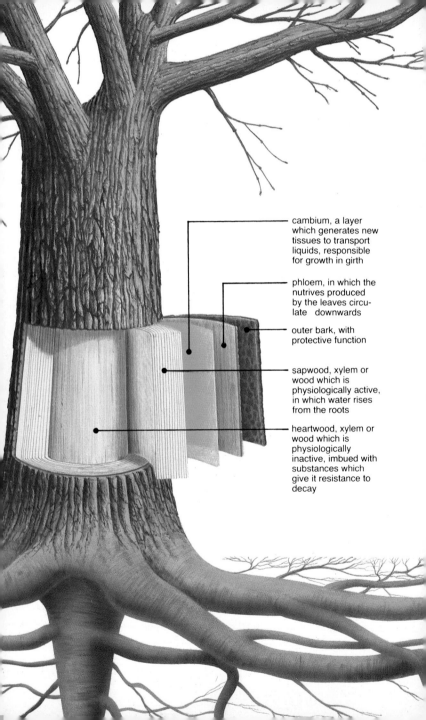

cambium, a layer which generates new tissues to transport liquids, responsible for growth in girth

phloem, in which the nutrives produced by the leaves circulate downwards

outer bark, with protective function

sapwood, xylem or wood which is physiologically active, in which water rises from the roots

heartwood, xylem or wood which is physiologically inactive, imbued with substances which give it resistance to decay

the bundle of embryonic or meristematic cells, ▶
small and cubical, distinguishable at the base of
this cross-section of leaf bud, responsible for
the growth of a shoot

◀ the layer of cells which forms the
cambium runs through the entire structure
of the tree, down to the smallest twigs,
generating wood (xylem) on the inside,
phloem on the outside

the bundle of ▶
small, cubical
embryonic cells,
distinguishable at
the tip of this
cross-section of
root apex, is
responsible for the
growth of the root
which anchors the
tree to the ground,
finds water there
and absorbs it
together with
dissolved mineral
salts

Bark. The outer layer of the tree consists of corky tissue which protects the inner wood from insects, drying out, and injury. It can vary in thickness – from a few millimeters to more than 12 inches (30 cm). It varies in appearance, differing with species and changing with age.

Cambium. Composed of a thin layer directly under the bark, it produces phloem and xylem cells and is responsible for increasing the girth of the trunk and branches. When the tree is injured or when a branch breaks off, cells in the cambium gradually form a scar-like callus which eventually covers the wound.

Sapwood. This is the part of the wood which performs two essential functions: upward transport of water and minerals and transport and storage of food produced by the leaves.

Heartwood. Frequently darker in color, this is the central part of stems and trunks and is composed of dead wood. Often darker than the surrounding wood because of a high concentration of resins, it gives firm support to the tree.

Leaves

These may be deciduous – destined to fall at the first sign of frost, having performed their annual function – or evergreen – lasting the entire winter. They differ morphologically according to species and are distinguished by their shape, arrangement on the stalk or branch, and by the number of parts into which they are divided. They are generally green, but may assume, due to the presence of red pigment, diverse shades from pinkish to reddish brown. When the percentage of chlorophyll – which gives the green coloration to the leaves – is low, they take on a golden, yellow or yellow streaked tone. No leaf is truly evergreen and its life varies from about six months to a year, exceptions being the needles of certain conifers which remain on the branch for several years.

The leaf could be described as the factory, the primal source of life, the first link in what is called the alimentary chain, which means that the sun's energy, captured and elaborated by the leaf, completes an infrangible whole when it once more turns into energy in its capacity as food for herbivorous animals, carnivores, and finally man. Leaf tissues through the process of photosynthesis form the organic compounds which will in due course break down, each performing its own task in the creation and maintenance of animal organisms. To perform these functions, unique upon earth, leaf tissues are highly specialized, being composed of cells containing various pigments; the most important of these, chlorophyll, is formed only in the presence of light. Chlorophyll is contained in green corpuscles, the chloroplasts, and has the property of capturing light energy and using it, by means of complex photochemical reactions, to convert carbon dioxide obtained from the atmosphere and added to the raw sap into organic compounds such as sugar and starch.

In addition to the taking in of carbon dioxide and the giving out of oxygen, much of the water collected by the roots is dispersed, by means of transpiration and respiration, into the air. This protects the leaves from excessive heat and permits the upward movement of sap. Once they have carried out their primary function, the leaves fall to the ground where they are decomposed by bacteria and fungi and thus enrich the soil with elements needed by the plant, in an autonomous and continuous cycle.

PHYSIOLOGY OF THE BONSAI

A bonsai is a normal tree whose development is not halted but rather guided in order to obtain a healthy dwarf tree. The wonderful mechanism of a normal tree has been broadly described. Now we shall see how bonsai development differs from this pattern.

Roots
In nature roots tend to develop according to necessity and opportunity, but, if a plant is confined to a small, shallow container, root growth will be restricted and top growth slowed down. This is how plants become *bonsai*. In a normal tree much of the root system serves to anchor it to the ground; as this is not required in a potted tree, bonsai roots can be drastically shortened. This root pruning is very important to promote a renewal process. By reducing the mass of roots in the pot, pruning provides space for young, vigorous roots to grow. It is new root hairs that absorb the water and minerals and give a healthy bonsai.

Trunk and branches
In nature, growth of the trunk and branches is determined by the tree's need to take the greatest possible advantage of sunlight and to overcome competition from other trees. Trunks lean because of the importance of wind, erosion, or physical damage. They are broad and tapering in pastures because there are no competitive trees growing nearby and the crown of the tree can spread, unhindered. Many low branches make the trunk broad at its base. An old tree has many surface roots because of erosion. Branches have finer and finer ramification as the result of many years of growth under good conditions. None of this happens with a potted plant unless the artist manipulates it through pruning, wiring, etc. Woody plants in small containers would just look like small shrubs if they were not skillfully handled by man because natural forces are not at work here.

Occasional selective trimming of the shoots and pruning of the branch tips will guarantee that the tree takes on a compact shape, the foliage being distributed according to the pattern we have in mind. A tangible result of the care a bonsai has received is the number of small ramifications among the branches themselves and the abundance of leaves.

The bark, distinct for each species, is a particularly important feature of a bonsai, and given the fact that it develops very gradually,

is one of the few elements indicative of the tree's age and worth.

As mentioned, the callus tissue produced by a tree is capable of covering, partially or entirely, the wounds caused by pruning or wiring of branches, counteracting any harmful effects.

Leaves

The size and arrangement of the leaves depend, among other things, on water and light, two important elements which have to be available in proper balance (see p. 26, photosynthetic process). There are no general formulas because needs vary from one species to another. It is worth remembering, nevertheless, that in order to obtain small and well distributed leaves, you should water sparingly and provide plenty of light. In theory this criterion applies above all to the period of spring reawakening, when the buds open and form new leaves. Defoliation is another technique used to produce small leaves. However, since this coincides with the time when the plant produces maximum effort, even utilizing some of its reserve substances, it is advisable to carry out defoliation (in deciduous species) at the beginning of summer, when the plant has replenished its stocks.

As a rule maximum plant growth occurs in the highest parts and in the terminal section of the lateral branches. This abundant growth of the tips can be exploited, in bonsai, in order to thicken the crown. Partial or total removal of the terminal twigs will temporarily halt growth in those areas but will stimulate vegetation where it is usually sparse, lower down, and towards the center of the plant.

The leaves are a sign that the tree is healthy. Rich, luxuriant growth indicates that, overall, it is in good shape, whereas the opposite warns of some shortcoming. In this respect the habit of deciduous species is typical, for if water is lacking the leaves tend to lose their stiffness. In conifers, on the other hand, the color of the needles becomes dull if the tree is ailing. Unfortunately these symptoms appear after prolonged abuse, so that countermeasures are more difficult and more urgent.

LIGHT

Light is the energy source of plants and this must always be borne in mind both when creating and maintaining a bonsai, because it determines the entire life of the tree. For example, if we look at nature, we see that plants of the same species which live under different light conditions develop leaves that vary considerably in size; those that live in shade or semi-shade normally have bigger leaves to maximize light absorbing surfaces, while those in full light often have much smaller leaves. In addition, trees growing in a dense forest tend to lose their lower branches, whereas a solitary tree does the same with those branches well hidden by the foliage. The reason for this behavior is easily explained: the tree produces vegetation where it can collect the maximum amount of light. If light is not equally distributed, growth will not be harmonious. The stimulus of light, in fact, also has an influence on the shape of the tree, causing a disproportionate lengthening of the more exposed branch cells as against those in shade (positive heliotropism). Not all trees, however, need the same quantity of light, nor does light invariably mean direct exposure to the sun's rays. We should not forget that exposure to strong sunlight increases transpiration in the leaves; when transpiration exceeds the availability of water, the leaves become partially or wholly dry, often with harmful consequences for the tree.

From this sketch of the forces that mold a tree in nature, it is easy to see that the following aesthetic guidelines for shaping bonsai, draw on observations of tree forms in the wild.

● the lowest branches should also be the longest;

● the other branches should become gradually shorter towards the apex;

● the branches should never directly overlap but be distributed along the axis of the trunk;

● it is a grave error to develop a branch from the inside of a curve;

● it is essential to remove any small branches which stem from the point where a branch meets the trunk or from the base of the branches.

These criteria correspond to the normal tree's growth habits and light requirements. Aesthetics is therefore not an end in itself but is linked to the physiology and good health of the bonsai.

SOIL

Every writer and virtually every bonsai enthusiast recommends his own type of potting mixture. Some claim to have found the ideal solution in an artificial mixture in which soil is not one of the components, while others look for complicated blends of earth and composts. In nature, soil determines plant growth; depending on its permeability, the presence or absence of water and of nutritive substances, growth can be stimulated, retarded, or even curtailed. In nature, plant roots can grow to where the soil is more satisfactory. The soil for potted plants, however, must fill all requirements in a small space.

The ideal growing medium must be properly aerated so as to allow circulation of oxygen and at the same time to hold sufficient water to satisfy the requirements of the plant between one application of water and another.

One mixture that can be recommended is based on good soil with the addition of 10 per cent clay, and coarse sand in proportions varying from a minimum of 20 per cent to a maximum of 40 per cent for conifers. The sand can be replaced by expanded clay, perlite or even pumice. All the materials added to the soil must be sieved to eliminate the tiniest particles.

Another method is to take ordinary garden soil and to pass it through two sieves of different meshes. The first sieving will retain the bigger lumps which can be used for drainage, the second will leave the basic soil for the growing medium that should be of an easy running consistency, and a third will yield the finest soil which can be used as a layer for growing moss on the surface. Although this is a practical method, it is inconvenient in that the average-sized part to be used as a growing medium will only be a small quantity compared with the total sieved.

The following remarks may help to find the right formula for our bonsai soil.

• The drainage will vary from one species to another, but it is important to bear in mind the surroundings where we and our plants live. If the climate is cool and airy, drainage will need to be better than in a climate where there is plenty of warm sunshine and hot summers.

• The plants live in symbiosis with mycorrhizae, with the thin, living threads, or hyphae, of the fungus entwined around the roots. Without close association with the proper fungi, growth will be impeded. It is therefore advisable to sprinkle a layer of the original earth over the lower part of the roots to ensure the proper mycorrhizae are mixed into the soil.

• All components of the growing medium must be well dried and left out for a few days in the sun. It should be turned occasionally to get rid of any parts of plants, seeds, larvae or insects which may find their way into it.

FERTILIZERS

There are several myths about bonsai cultivation which are not easy to correct. One school of thought maintains that bonsai plants should be kept constantly on the brink of collapse; at the other extreme there are those who insist on over-feeding their bonsai in the belief that this will keep all possible evils at bay. In actual fact, fertilizing a bonsai means paying great attention to the specific needs of the plant at each stage of its growth, providing it with the right substances at the right moment.

Although it is true that the elements necessary for the plant's growth come from water, the air, and the soil, it is equally true that bonsai plants do not always, indeed seldom, find optimum conditions for survival inside their pot. Fertilizers make it possible to help each and every plant cope with less-than-ideal conditions. They may be either chemical or organic and the elements they contain are divided into macroelements and microelements or trace elements. The macroelements – nitrogen (chemical symbol N), phosphorus (P), and potassium (K) – are so called because they are utilized in large quantities by the plant, while the microelements – magnesium (Mg), boron (B), zinc (Zn), manganese (Mn), calcium (Ca), iron (Fe), copper (Cu), cobalt (Co), and molybdenum (Mn) – are necessary only in small amounts. Although various elements are necessary to plant growth and function, in incorrect amounts they may also inhibit them. It is therefore advisable to resort to prepared complete fertilizers. Application should take into account both the season and the species. In spring, fertilizer containing mainly nitrogen will encourage leaf growth, while a bigger proportion of potassium, in autumn, will sustain structural development. Plants with flowers and fruits, on the other hand, need to be given a feed with a high concentration of phosphorus in early spring or before flowering.

As is the case with soil, there are diverse opinions on fertilizers, and one frequent dilemma is whether a chemical feed is preferable to an organic one, or vice versa. The initial response may come from a consideration of the time it takes the plant to assimilate the active principles in the feed. Whereas chemical fertilizers are assimilated quickly, organic fertilizers are generally slow-acting and need one or two months before they are available to the plant. On the other hand, a specific organic feed for bonsai, even though it may not be easy to find, never yields unpleasant surprises.

Certain principles should be paramount when selecting and using fertilizers:

- study the specific needs of the plant;
- program the fertilizer application, bearing in mind that an organic feed has to be given at least a month earlier than a chemical one;
- if transplanting, and consequently a change of soil, is to be carried out systematically every year, the risks of using chemical fertilizers are diminished;
- frequent watering tends to remove nutritive substances: it is advisable, therefore, to repeat applications of fertilizer in spring and autumn

which, in the case of chemical feeds, should be given every two weeks;
• do not feed at the hottest time of year (generally from mid July to early September);
• chemical feeds should be administered in half the dose recommended by the makers. Solid organic fertilizer, if used, should be applied only twice a year, at the start of regrowth and at the end of summer.

HORMONES

Hormones are the chemicals that coordinate the activities of the plant, some stimulating growth and others inhibiting. Synthetic substances are now manufactured to be used as growth regulators. Although there are no specific works on hormones which stimulate the rooting of bonsai plants, this does not justify the fears and doubts on the subject that are often voiced, even by experts in the field. The best known hormones which encourage vegetative growth found on sale, are synthetic products which perform the same action as natural auxins. It is essential to follow the makers' instructions.

Time is a determining factor for successful transplanting. Even when this is carried out with extreme care, any mutilation of the root apparatus will cause a degree of suffering to the plant and a temporary halt to the vegetative cycle, though not to transpiration. A hormone compound helps to form scar tissue on the cut roots, makes it easier for them to re-form and develop anew, and diminishes the risks of transplanting, giving the plant the chance to recover its full functions as quickly as possible.

There are two recommended ways of using these substances.

When potting or repotting plants with their ball of soil, water the transplant the day beforehand and immediately afterwards with water in which the hormone rooting powder has been dissolved. In this case the new soil can be made to adhere by gently shaking the pot and using a stick to fill in any holes, thus avoiding having to touch any of the damp soil clinging to the roots.

If the plant has bare roots, however, it is best to soak the root system in the solution, letting it stand overnight and carrying out the transplant the following day according to the normal procedures. When this is done, give an application of the same water in which the plant was kept overnight. The hormones, diluted in water, soon lose their efficacy, so it is important to transplant within 24 hours. It is also advisable to water again at least twice after ten days.

WATERING

Accounts by famous masters such as John Naka tend to give the impression that success in growing bonsai, both for beginners and experts, depends on watering. I recall that when I first came across the booklet by Zeho Nakamura, subtitled *Quick and Easy*, and read that the author watered as frequently as seven times a day, I got a shock and feared my days as a bonsaist were numbered.

No matter how well-positioned the bonsai is, pay great attention to its watering. Trees in the wild take up water from nearby soil but then have access to any source in the surrounding earth. Bonsai, in the confined space of a pot do not have this scope and will not survive any length of time without water.

Tap water contains too much calcium and chlorine so rainwater is to be preferred. If only tap water is available, then stand a can of it at room temperature for 24 hours so the chlorine is dispersed into the air and the water becomes clear. This way the water will also be at the right temperature, not too hot or cold from the tap. Sulfur dioxide in the atmosphere can damage the foliage so spray the leaves with water periodically to clean them. Do this when the sun is not directly on them. Trees with *jin* should not be sprayed too often to avoid risk of rotting.

Experience will tell you how often to water, but look at the plant, test the soil with the finger, and see how much the pot weighs. In summer, or in hot, dry or windy weather, it may be necessary to water twice a day, once in the early morning and once in the evening, when the sun is not so hot. In winter, or in cool, cloudy, and humid weather, the trees will be less active and one watering should suffice, ideally later in the morning when the soil is not frozen and the temperature is higher. Deciduous trees take more water in summer than evergreens; conifers have specialized leaves that retain more water. In winter the deciduous tree is resting and needs little water while the conifer, still growing a little, uses water. Pines can tolerate dry soil but fine-leaved deciduous trees need much watering in hot weather.

Watering should be thorough as a damp surface does not mean the pot is wet through. Sprinkle water from a can into the pot or submerge the pot up to, but not over, the rim into a bowl of water for a couple of minutes and take it out when the surface soil is soaked. Over-watering is as big a problem as under-watering so take care not to risk rotting the roots. Only lake- or river-side trees, such as willows, alders, and swamp cypresses, will tolerate longer immersion. Conifers in general need good drainage and pines in particular develop root rot easily.

CHOOSING A PLANT

The choice of a plant to create a bonsai may seem easy but is in fact quite difficult. In the first place you have to decide whether the plant to be chosen has the necessary characteristics to be transformed into a bonsai. Nobody, not even the greatest master, can create a masterpiece from the wrong sort of plant, selected at random. To be guided by first impulse often means spending money on something which, after closer perusal, you may regret having bought. Unless you have the courage to throw it out or the nerve to give away as a present something that will never make a bonsai, you will end up with a constant reminder of your mistake.

Never be impatient when choosing a plant. Examine it and examine it again, weighing up every feature. Although it may seem a waste of time, you will be amply rewarded when you see the finished results.

It is important to bear in mind that a bonsai should be something pleasingly harmonious, with leaves, flowers, and fruits in suitable proportion to the overall size. While the size of leaves or needles may in time be somewhat reduced, this is impossible with flowers and fruit. A normal-sized fruit on a tree that is some 8 in (20 cm) in height may arouse curiosity but will produce an inharmonious result, wholly undesirable in a bonsai.

The following are the points to look for when purchasing bonsai material.

Roots. These should spread out radially from the base of the trunk. The presence of thick roots at the base is of primary importance because it helps to give an appearance of maturity to the plant. Even if there are not surface roots, the basal part of the trunk should be the thickest.

Trunk. It is essential that this should taper. Avoid trunks which get broader with height and which have unsightly nodes, bumps or graft unions. Bear in mind that you can always shorten it, forming a new tip with a lateral branch. The trunk should display the typical bark of the species or at least signs of bark.

Branches. In order to achieve proper balance, these should start at about one third the total height of the plant. The lowest branch, no matter whether positioned left or right of the trunk, must also be the most important; the second, higher up, should be on the opposite side to the first; the third should be between the first and second branch at the back of the plant. This third branch, smaller than the other two, should be off-center towards the left or right, so that its front part can be seen.

The first three branches give the tree its character and posture, and this pattern should be followed by the other branches which become smaller and shorter towards the top. One of the most frequent errors is to retain bigger branches higher up. It is always better to have a plant with smaller but properly balanced branches than one with large branches that are clearly unbalanced. If the trunk is slightly sinuous, make sure that there are branches on the outside of the curves.

The branches also play an important role when choosing a front view: no main branch on the lower part of the trunk, which forms the ideal center of gravity in the composition of the pot, should point directly towards the observer.

These are of course broad guidelines and do not rule out other possible variations founded on deeper knowledge and experience of bonsai styles.

A final hint: use indigenous plants, at least for your first bonsai. Plants raised outside their native area pose difficulties which beginners, at any rate, would be ill-advised to tackle.

REPOTTING

Repotting is without doubt an important operation in the life of a plant, for it has a major influence on its state of health.

Any gardener knows that all pot plants have to be repotted from time to time. Whereas normally we just replace the container with a bigger one, adding some soil, in the case of bonsai this is usually not desirable. The small pot is necessary to restrict growth and provide a harmonious frame for the artistic tree.

From time to time, remove any roots hanging over the rim or out of the bottom of the pot. If the root system is well developed this may be an opportunity to shorten, if need be, the tap-root and thick lateral roots, coating the cuts with a sealing compound.

It is hard to lay down general rules for repotting. With conifers it is usually carried out every two to three years, with deciduous and evergreen species every year or two. Bonsai grown in warmer climates will need more frequent repotting than those grown in colder zones (compare every 2–3 years in a temperate climate to every 5 years in a cool climate). A fairly reliable indication is to keep a close watch on the development of the leaves over the year; plenty of healthy leaves during the growing season points to an abundance of healthy roots.

Prepare the pot by covering the drainage holes with mesh and passing a wire through the holes to anchor the plant into the container. To ensure drainage, cover the bottom of the container with coarse sand and spread over this a thin layer of soil. At this point, position the plant, gently fasten the wire to the base of the trunk and carefully fill the space between roots and pot with new, well dried soil. If necessary use a small stick, to eliminate air pockets. Work the soil around the roots finally pressing the soil down by hand. Sometimes the tree will stand firmly enough in the pot without the help of wires. Most trees, however, will need to be anchored. After repotting, water abundantly with a fine spray.

BASIC TECHNIQUES

If you watch a demonstration, the transformation of an ordinary plant into a bonsai may seem to be a sleight of hand, and I am of the opinion that such a display is liable to encourage the false impression that little time is needed to effect such a transformation. But despite this risk, it is the only way of teaching how to handle a plant. Having expressed this point of view, it remains to explain the procedure as simply as possible.

Pruning
Shaping a plant into a bonsai is to recreate the image of a tree in miniature proportions both by pruning the branches and by trimming the new shoots.

How to repot a bonsai. 1–2: Screens are placed above the drainage holes. A wire is then threaded through the screens to attach the plant to the container. 3: Fine soil (A), medium-sized potting soil (B), coarse sand placed at the bottom of the container to assist drainage (C). 4–5: The plant is positioned in the pot and a stick is used to work the growing mixture firmly around the roots. 6–7: Smoothing the surface soil with a brush and a final watering.

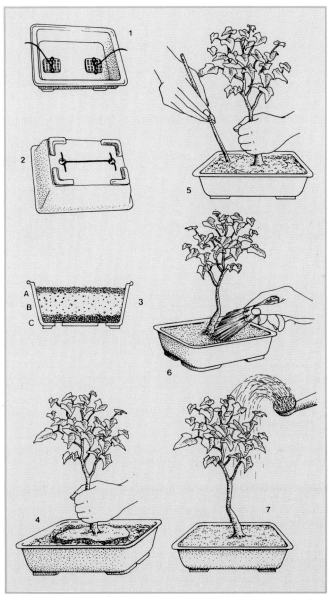

The first major act of selective pruning – i.e. choosing the main branches – needs to be done during the plant's rest season so as to avoid shocks at critical moments. The branches will be cut according to the imaginary design you have of the finished tree. Should you be in any doubt as to what shape is required, try displaying the trunk at various angles, raising one edge of the pot with a wedge of wood, so as to find what looks best. If you want to visualize the eventual effect of pruning a branch, cover it with a piece of newspaper or take a photograph and snip the section off. If after all this you are still unable to reach a satisfactory decision, it is best to leave it for another time. As happens so frequently in life, the solution may be close at hand although not always easy to see.

As we have discussed, the tree has a front, a back, and two sides. Obviously you will decide to work from the front, while at the same time modifying the sides, so that their effect is equally pleasing and harmonious. To remove a branch, make a clean cut with a pair of concave pruners so as to remove a portion of underlying wood at the same time. To shorten a branch, however, simply make a slanting cut. If you want to create a new apex, leave a shoot on the lower surface of a lateral branch and a frontal shoot on the trunk; in this way there will be shoots in ideal positions, once vegetative growth is resumed, to form the new tips.

In the case of deciduous and broadleaved evergreen trees one can take advantage of the adventitious shoots which form after pruning; however, for conifers it is safer to shorten the branches only when

The photographs illustrate the successive phases in shaping a nursery plant into a bonsai. From left to right: the plant before work starts; cutting back the crown and positioning the trunk; positioning the branches and cutting back the roots; the plant in the bonsai tray.

strong shoots or, even better, lateral twigs, are visible. Provided the lateral twigs look strong and healthy, it is possible to reduce the length of the branches, cutting off the current year's vegetation.

For trimming to shape, the tender new shoots can be pinched with the nails, leaving just a pair of leaflets at the tip of the branch. This operation may be repeated throughout the growing season. But if the aim is to develop a branch, it must be left undisturbed until it has reached the desired size, then shortened and set in position.

As regards conifers, the apical shoot – as a rule the biggest, situated in the center of the branch tip – is removed in autumn. In spring, when formation of the new needles is barely visible, three quarters of the shoots should be removed, holding them firmly between thumb and index finger, and using the same fingers of the other hand to detach them with a sharp rotating movement.

Potting and Repotting
The first secret in the construction of a bonsai is, as we have seen, choosing the right plant. If it is potted, the base of the trunk and lateral surface roots are exposed, the tap-root – usually the central root and almost the continuation of the trunk – is shortened, and the side roots are spread out horizontally; this in practice reduces the overall length of the roots by about two thirds. Then, having freed the trunk and the thicker roots of all unnecessary side roots, it is a matter only of pruning or positioning the branches and the tree will have entered upon its new phase as a bonsai. If, in the course of a demonstration, positioning,

39

fastening, and transplanting are as a rule done at the same time, for everyday purposes it is far better to position the branches during the next annual growth cycle.

Often, however, things are rather less simple. In many plants the roots are so long that it is impossible to shorten them safely in one stage. In such cases, you should merely trim most of the tap-root, sacrificing as few as possible of the thinner roots which should be spread out in a new container. Wait for a complete growth cycle and then repeat the operation, continuing to repeat it – a bonsai never responds to impatience – until all the roots are contained in a ball of soil more or less as thick as the diameter of the trunk base. Heap the earth around this, but not above the height of the pot. All these operations need to be carried out at the right season which varies, according to climate and species, from early to late spring and from early to late autumn. There are no hard and fast rules in this respect but it is worth remembering that the term ''spring'' is not necessarily the season which commences on 21 March but rather the moment when vegetative growth is resumed and buds begin to swell. Autumn is thus the period when the leaves begin to change color and shrivel prior to falling.

Having discussed these problems with friends who live both in northern and southern regions of Europe, it is evident how different climatic conditions can affect the time for transplanting. Whereas in the north it is definitely preferable to carry out this operation in spring, because of the gradual rise in temperature, in the south it is better to wait until autumn because temperatures on spring days are often too high and can prove harmful.

In transforming plants into bonsai we should observe a few rules which, although not a guarantee of success, certainly make it attainable.

• Get rid of all branches and twigs that are not necessary to the final design of the tree.

• When transplanting broadleafed evergreens and at the same time drastically pruning the roots, remove all the leaves, retaining only the stalks. This will avoid excessive transpiration during the critical period of rooting.

• Keep newly repotted plants sheltered from wind and direct sunlight and make sure they are firmly set in the container. Failing this, attach the trunk with soft cord to the four sides of the pot. After transplanting, soak the plant abundantly, either by top-watering or immersing it.

• Build, if need be, a rudimentary miniature greenhouse with two steel wires bent in a U-shape, fixed crosswise, and covered with a sheet of polythene. Remember to spray at least twice a day, and keep the plant in the shade until it has recovered.

• Should the height of the plant threaten to loosen it, give it a stiff support (stake), attaching it to the container and the trunk.

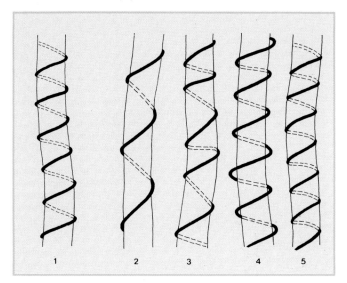

WIRING

The technique of positioning or shaping the trunk and branches with metal wire comes from Japan, and since their trees have reached such perfection, it is sensible for every bonsaist to understand how to carry out this operation.

There are two types of wire, of different diameters, which are used everywhere: aluminium wire – anodized so as to blend better with the trunk and avoid oxidization – and copper wire, used after being softened and oxidized in fire. The main difference between these two types is in their malleability. The former is the more flexible and thus decidedly easier to handle, even by beginners, while the latter, especially in larger measures, is stiffer. Aluminium wire is easy to remove and immediately reusable whereas copper wire becomes even harder after bending and cannot be reused; large diameter wire will need cutting to be removed. Copper, especially when thinner wire is required, holds the position better but it is not always easy to find all the measures of wire needed. It is also more expensive. Aluminium wire comes in larger diameters and is therefore more visible. When all is said and done, the choice is likely to be dictated, not by any rules, but by personal inclination.

To modify the development of the trunk, the wire is threaded through the roots of the base, and wound around the back of the tree (p. 42, fig. 1). To shape the branches, the wire is either attached to two opposite branches or anchored to the base of one branch and tied to

Three methods of fixing the wire in different situations. Wire threaded through the soil, parallel to the trunk and from the back of the plant (1). Wire fixed to the trunk to position two branches placed at different heights (2). Wire attached to the trunk to position a branch (3).

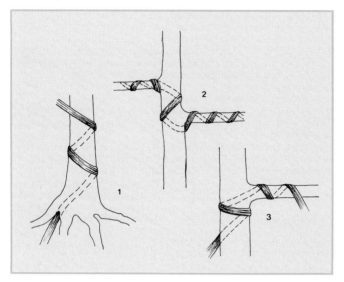

the trunk (p. 42, fig. 2–3). Once the wire is attached it is wound in regular spirals so that it adheres firmly but gently to the trunk or branch. Care must be taken to follow the same direction as that in which the trunk or branch will eventually be bent as the wire will tighten round them. The spirals should be even, not be too close nor too far apart, neither too many nor too few. "Right is right" remarked John Naka, during one demonstration. With a little experience, wiring is never a great problem. As always, practice, rather than theory, makes perfect.

Here are some ways of avoiding errors and utilizing wire to the best advantage.

● Never use wire on plants which are not growing strongly.

● Choose wire of the greatest possible diameter in relation to the trunk or branch to be shaped. If you do not get the desired effect, add another wire parallel to the first.

● Coil the wire directly around the bark, taking care not to cover twigs, petioles, leaves, needles or shoots.

● Do not water, especially in the case of trees with delicate bark, for at least 8–10 hours before wiring.

● Keep a constant watch on the wire and shift it as soon as it shows signs of cutting into the bark.

● After completion of the wiring, allow the tree to remain in shade or in a sheltered spot for a couple of weeks.

When working on trees with particularly fragile bark, the Japanese advise bandaging the wire. This is a difficult and laborious operation, but either of the two following methods can be recommended. Bind the trunk or branch, especially those parts that need drastic bending, with a strip of cotton or raffia prior to applying the wire, or insert the wire, before use, into transparent plastic tubing which is commercially available in various sizes. Neither solutions are ideal aesthetically, but they are preferable to ugly scars, especially as they do not have to be kept in place for too long.

Shaping the trunk and branches does not necessarily have to be done with wire. There are, in fact, a number of alternative techniques: weights attached to the branches, ties fixed to the pot, levers, jacks, stakes, and so forth.

The best times to carry out these operations are spring and winter, depending on the plant species and the flexibility of the branches. If, as often happens, the result is not completely satisfactory, the shaping procedure can be repeated, leaving the tree to rest for an entire growth cycle.

MOSS

Moss is a sound compliment to bonsai, providing an attractive simulation of green undergrowth. There are many species in different colors ranging from yellowish to bright green. Moreover, they differ in size and height. The softer and brighter-colored mosses are the best for using with bonsai. In the famous Saiho-ji garden at Kyoto in Japan, mosses constitute the ground cover and have the consistency of a soft green carpet.

Whereas, with the exception of some tiny ferns or a few houseleeks, weeds should be kept out of a bonsai container, mosses are not only acceptable but worth looking for. Because they only have small, superficial root-like structures called rhizoids they do not disturb or take away food from the tree roots and they fulfill the important function of keeping the soil moist. During watering they prevent any earth being lost, acting as sponges by absorbing water and then releasing it in warm weather.

There are two methods of using moss: collecting it in layers and pressing it firmly to the top of the soil, or allowing it to dry and "sowing" it by crumbling it over the surface. If required, moss can also be kept, after being dried, in sealed containers or, even better, carefully "seeded" in a cool, moist spot. The latter method is better because the moss will then look more natural and form a compact cover of greenery. Sowing should be preceded by abundant watering and followed by spraying. It is advisable to cover the earth with a sheet of clear plastic. In a week or so growth will already be visible.

JIN AND SHARI

In Japanese, *jin* is the dead part of a plant. To understand what is meant, have a look at some of the older trees in high mountain

The famous Saiho-ji (Moss Temple) garden, at Kyoto, Japan, where the compact moss forms a soft green carpet.

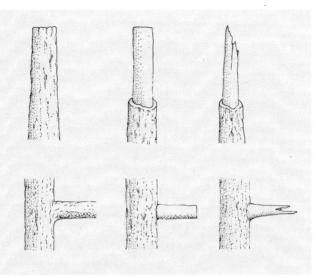

regions. The top of the tree and some of the lateral branches will often display areas stripped of bark which natural adversities have turned silvery. *Jin* is normally used either to shorten the trunk or to create a point of interest where a branch, for aesthetic reasons, has been removed. To obtain *jin*, make a cut across the bark at the base of the branch or the top of the tree so as to reveal the inner wood. Shorten to the required length and, using a pair of pruning shears, split and remove the bark with a rotational movement. You then shape the point so that it does not appear to be cut off but modeled by natural events (see p. 46).

A variant of *jin* is *shari*, which is achieved by extending the cut down the trunk. These techniques should only be carried out on trees with hard, resinous wood strong enough to guarantee lasting effects.

Both *jin* and *shari* are best done during the tree's active growth period, when the bark comes off more easily. Soon afterwards, if required, you can position the parts with wire, which can be removed when the decorticated section is dry. It is a good idea to smear the edges of the bark with a sealing compound (also known as Japanese cut-wound paste or grafting wax) to help scar formation.

Shari is the basis of the Sharimiki style, in which a large part of the tree is stripped of bark, except for one or two branches and a strip of intact bark joining these branches. This style is recommended particularly when the rest of the tree is not of special interest as a bonsai or when it does not taper suitably from base to apex. When working on the stripped part, it is advisable to carry out the whole operation

immediately, for otherwise the wood, as it dries, may harden and make things more difficult.

A variation of the Sharimiki style is to insert a live plant into an interesting dry trunk used as a base. The latter must first be treated with a wood preservative and then kept for six months or so in the open air. When all is ready, arrange the base and make a channel slightly bigger than the diameter of the live plant, from which all the branches on one side have been removed. Wedge this into the dry wood so that only a portion of the trunk protrudes. Then make two, deep, vertical cuts in the live trunk with a sharp knife so as to stimulate the formation of scar tissue which will swell and cover the junction of the two trunks. Seal this with a suitable sealing compound and tie the two parts firmly with raffia. Provided the operation is done skillfully, after a couple of years the bark of the live plant will jut out slightly from the trunk.

Two pieces of advice: use the same or very similar types of wood; and follow the veining of the dry trunk.

To get a more interesting effect and to avoid the dead parts rotting, it is worth applying lime sulfur solution with a brush, taking care not to touch the living parts and covering the soil in the pot with a sheet of plastic so that no liquid seeps down to the roots. This operation should preferably be carried out in the warmer months when the parts have completely dried out, repeated a month later and then as needed for at least a couple of years. Eventually the treated parts will take on an attractive silvery white color.

Shari *is the basis of the* Sharimiki *style, which features specially treated dry wood (see description of this style on p. 71).*
Juniperus rigida (Sharimiki style).

ENLARGING THE TRUNK

The tapering of the trunk is one of the many valued features of a bonsai. A beautifully formed base and strong surface roots combine to give it an appearance of elegance and age. Consequently, enlargement of the trunk and development of the surface roots are often prime objectives of the bonsaist, and sometimes achieved very successfully.

In my view, there are two effective ways of enlarging the trunk which will yield satisfactory, if not spectacular, results. The first is to puncture the bark to the depth of the wood at several key points with a large needle; the second is to hammer it firmly and decisively without removing the bark. These procedures, by disturbing the most active part of the tree, provoke a reaction likely to enlarge the trunk at the required point, but never more than one quarter of its circumference. Attaching some damp moss, held in place by raffia, to the treated part will encourage a good result.

There are also various ways of tackling the base. The simplest is to keep the plant in a spacious pot in which it can grow freely until the desired results are obtained. At each repotting, lift the surface roots and set a flat stone at the base so as to prevent further development at that point.

An almost similar procedure, but only for younger plants, is to extend the roots over a flat surface in which a number of holes have been pierced (the bottom of a discarded terracotta pot is ideal). This barrier will enable both the surface roots and the base of the trunk to grow.

Some trees, such as Japanese maples or olives, can develop interesting bases. To encourage this tendency and to make it a focal point, the roots directly underneath the trunk must be cut away at each repotting. In time this will enlarge the base of the trunk.

INDOOR BONSAI

These are essentially species from tropical and subtropical countries which manage to adapt to indoor conditions. In response to the increasing interest in raising bonsai – particularly indoors – such species are now commercially available. Unfortunately, as there is often a lack of knowledge in looking after these plants, they frequently lead to disappointing results.

While agreeing that nothing can be a real substitute for the tree's original climate, I still maintain that with a little goodwill, a minimum of equipment, and a good dose of common sense, virtually any type of bonsai from tropical or subtropical regions can be treated as a house plant and kept healthy.

Apart from optimal temperatures, which range, depending on the species, from around 45° to 75°F (7° to 24°C), the principal aims are to provide adequate humidity and light.

In the case of tropical species only, a room which reproduces the conditions of a greenhouse would be ideal as far as humidity goes. A large container of water placed on the veranda or in front of a window will, as it evaporates, provide such moisture.

With respect to light – and remember that some tropical species need as much as 12 hours daily – the first thing when buying the tree is to ascertain its requirements. It may then be necessary to install one or more special lights which illuminate the plants every day for the same length of time. The temperature should be allowed to fall about 8°–10°F (4°–5°C) at night, with at least eight hours of darkness.

Subtropical or Mediterranean species can be equally demanding with regard to relative humidity, temperature, and light, particularly when grown in northern climates. It is essential at all times to give them a well-lit position close to a window, away from draughts, and to spray the foliage sufficiently so as to prevent excessive transpiration in the dry heat of the home. Artificial light is useful but not indispensable.

The amount of care required by these plants likewise depends on latitude. In northern Europe and the United States species such as *Olea europaea* and *Ficus carica* are considered house plants, whereas in the south they can live quite comfortably outside, although they are vulnerable to low temperatures.

Indoor bonsai follow the progression of seasons according to their species, although they tend to have a longer growing period. Evergreens, which never become completely dormant, should be fed moderately during the winter as well. Repotting will be done every year in early spring for subtropical and Mediterranean species, during the summer for tropical species.

In summer, for at least a couple of months, it is a good idea to expose the bonsai to fresh air and sunlight; this should be done gradually. And at all times avoid spraying or watering with cold tap water; this must always be warmed to the surrounding temperature to avoid any shock to the plants.

THE CONTAINER

The container and plant together should create a harmonious effect, so the pot has to be proportionate to the plant's shape and size. A pot that is too small will make everything look unbalanced and unstable, while if it is too big it will not show off the plant to full advantage.

The length of the container should be about two thirds the height of the plant and the width slightly less than the front and back projection of the branches. Its height should measure about the same as the diameter of the trunk at the base, except in the case of cascade or semi-cascade forms which require deep pots.

The position of the tree in the container, if the latter is oval or rectangular, can be calculated by dividing the length of the pot in half and the width into thirds. The trunk of the tree – in order to balance the

How to position a tree in a bonsai container. See detailed descriptions on pp. 50–52.

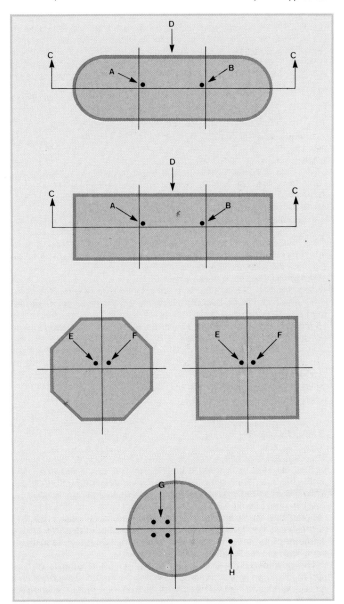

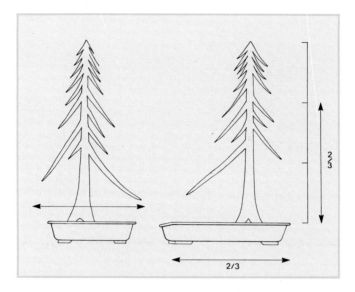

projection of the longest branch – is off-center in positions A and B, and the growth of the plant will, for the most part, be in position C; the trunk must never touch the rear rim of the pot (D). With round, hexagonal and square containers, the pot should be divided into quarters and the trunk will begin in positions E or F, slightly off-center towards the back. Again the exceptions are the cascade and semi-cascade forms, which should be planted on the opposite side to that which they overhang (G or H).

Bonsai pots come in an almost unlimited range of shapes and colors. They may be round, square, hexagonal, roundish with many corners, oval or rectangular. The height may vary from as little as ½ in (1 cm) to as much as 8 in (20 cm). Choice will be determined by various factors: The style, the development of the branches, the predominant color of the trunk and the leaves, and the tones of the flowers and fruits. Whereas in the past the preference was for containers in bright colors, painted or even in bas-relief, the trend today is towards plainer lines and softer colors. Sometimes a flat or concave slab of stone is used instead of a pot.

As a rule, unglazed pot colors are brown, reddish brown or gray for evergreens and conifers, while glazed containers in deep or pastel shades are preferred for flowering and fruiting species. In the latter instance the pot should enhance the predominant colors of the plant.

By and large, however, it is all a matter of personal taste. We can take into account how a pot can help to alter the overall appearance by experimenting with different containers for the same plant. If we have

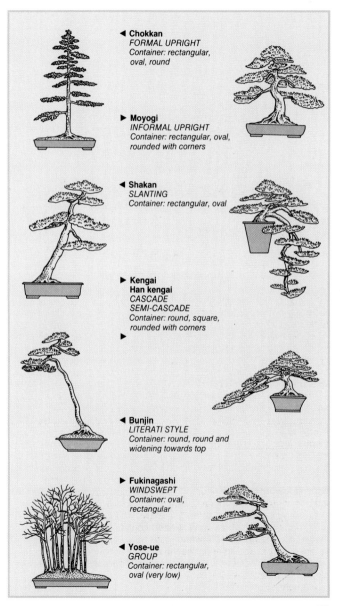

◀ **Chokkan**
FORMAL UPRIGHT
Container: rectangular,
oval, round

▶ **Moyogi**
INFORMAL UPRIGHT
Container: rectangular, oval,
rounded with corners

◀ **Shakan**
SLANTING
Container: rectangular, oval

▶ **Kengai**
Han kengai
CASCADE
SEMI-CASCADE
Container: round, square,
rounded with corners
▶

◀ **Bunjin**
LITERATI STYLE
Container: round, round and
widening towards top

▶ **Fukinagashi**
WINDSWEPT
Container: oval,
rectangular

◀ **Yose-ue**
GROUP
Container: rectangular,
oval (very low)

53

Three examples of ancient Chinese pots dating back to the Ching dynasty. (Author's collection.)

to vary the optimal proportion (plant to pot), it is always better to use a slightly bigger, rather than a smaller, container.

In conclusion, it is worth recalling that the history of pots goes back many centuries, spanning the period from the Ming dynasty (1465) to the present day, and that there is a market for them just as there is for the bonsai. The most valuable pots, both Chinese and Japanese, are genuine antiques, and accordingly fetch high prices both in Japan and abroad.

EQUIPMENT

It may well be true, as one of my bonsai friends maintains, that you can do everything, or almost everything, with a pair of modified electrician's pliers. It depends on what is to be done, how you want to do it, and on your personal ability and dexterity. Using the wide range of bonsai tools produced by the Japanese certainly does make things easier, however, and there is an undeniable pleasure in handling these beautiful instruments.

Two tools which even the beginner cannot do without are: concave branch-cutters which leave a cut that eventually closes without leaving a pronounced bump on the trunk, and wire-cutters with a long handle which reach right into the center of the foliage.

For operations ranging from the lopping of large branches to the snipping of leaves, there are numerous types of scissors and shears.

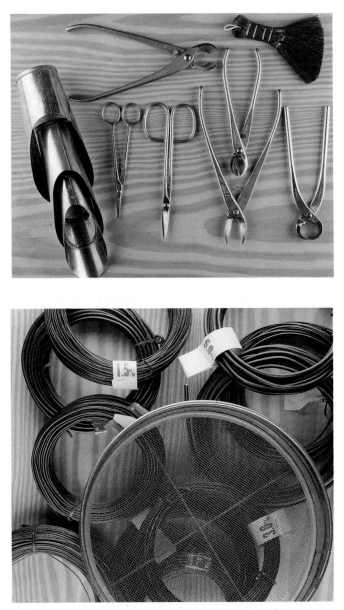

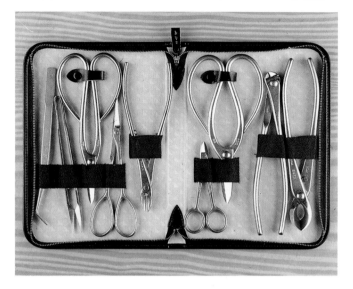

Dry or over-sized branches, however, should always be removed with a small pruning saw and trimmed with a chisel or the concave scissors.

Wire should be fixed with long-handled pliers and tweezers. Pliers bent out of alignment will serve to create *jin* and *shari*, and a series of sharp nippers will cut the roots cleanly without squashing them.

Other tools and sundries that can be considered are: a supply of different-sized meshing for sieving the soil and drainage material; wooden gouges in various sizes; a rake for the roots; watering cans or hoses fitted with a very fine spray; bamboo canes; and palm-fiber brushes, useful for cleaning the moss as well as cleaning and leveling the soil surface during repotting.

Another particularly useful accessory is a revolving turntable which can move freely or be clamped into position, so that the plant can be turned around to see and work on the different angles.

Mention has already been made of wire, with diameters that vary from ⅛ to ¼ in (0.3 to 0.6 mm). Keep an assortment on hand and remember, the more visible they are the less attractive the overall effect.

In recent years masters such as John Naka, Dan Robinson, and Masahiko Kimura have used small mechanical cutters, electric routers, and power saws for their demonstrations. The results, undeniably fascinating, involve techniques and tools that not only require precise knowledge of the limitations of the plants being used, but also great technical expertise. These techniques are not for every plant nor for every enthusiast.

Suiseki – *from Japanese sui, water, and seki, stone* – *often provide an accompaniment to bonsai, with their strong evocation of natural scenery or an object associated with nature. The stones are usually laid out on a specially built base and must all be natural. In this photograph the stone resembles a mountain chain.* (Author's collection.)

SHOWS AND JUDGING CRITERIA

It may seem unnecessary to talk about shows and judging criteria, given that bonsai ought to be based more on the pleasure of "doing" than that of "exhibiting" or "possessing." But there are two good reasons for taking part in such shows. Direct comparison with others can spur and enrich your efforts; moreover, shows help to spread the gospel of bonsai – encouraging the formation of societies and providing a pleasant opportunity for enthusiasts to get together.

A tree should be exhibited only when it is in peak shape. All plants have their "magic moment" in the course of a year, usually in spring when the flowers appear and the new, soft green foliage provides a pleasing contrast to the old trunks, or in autumn when the leaves take on spectacular colors and the branches are further adorned with attractive fruit.

An exhibition tree must carry a label with both the scientific and common name and preferably a rough indication as to the number of years it has been cultivated. Although it should be clear, from what has already been said, that the age of the tree is not a determining factor in itself for a bonsai, even if it impresses the uninitiated. Only when a tree shows all the characteristics of maturity – secondary branches, bark, and external roots – is its value and merit thereby increased.

Various attempts have been made, at international level as well, to apply a common criterion of judgement through a table that awards marks for the various points of the plant, with a view to creating a universal standard for appraising and defining a bonsai.

A typical table awards marks as follows:

20 marks for the artistic and overall effect

15 marks for the base of the trunk and arrangement of the surface roots

15 marks for the arrangement of the branches, their shape, and the density of secondary ramifications

15 marks for the structure of the trunk, the taper, and the characteristics of the bark

15 marks for the precision of the pruning, the wiring, and the position of the plant in the pot

15 marks for the presentation, the health of the plant, the moss or the surface compost

5 marks for the miniaturization of the leaves

TOTAL: **100** marks

The prevailing tendency is to use these criteria only for instructional purposes. I agree with this view because I do not think it possible to reconcile cold mathematical calculations with creativity. I am convinced that a bonsaist, above all, must know the specific needs of a plant, comply with them, proceed in accordance with the general principles of bonsai techniques, and finally put a personal stamp on the work which combines taste, inventiveness, and sensitivity.

There have been countless discussions in different places on the requirements and overall appearance of a bonsai, and no exact solutions have been found. The big question that remains is whether a bonsai should be a faithful reflection of a tree of the same species growing in the wild or whether it should simply be an imaginary plant.

My own opinion is that a bonsai, apart from recreating the image of a miniature tree, should evoke the same sensations as the original; more than just reflecting reality it should make our imagined tree seem real.

Just as every person has his or her own individuality and character, so every bonsai should have its own appearance and personality. Whereas no two people, however similar, are exactly alike, so too a bonsai has to differ from another in tiny details, in which it is possible to discern the handiwork of its creator.

Although the great Japanese masters have frequently invited us in the West to create new forms, taking our inspiration from nature which surrounds us, it is nevertheless true that a tree is a tree all over the world and that the Japanese have run the full gamut of possible classes and styles. Familiarity with such styles is the basic stock-in-trade of every bonsaist. However, this does not imply that we should slavishly ape them, no matter how praiseworthy the originals, with endless and often futile repetitions, leaving no scope for creativity.

The division into classes has been established on the basis of height, number of trees in a container, and number of trunks on the same tree. Height is always measured in a straight line from the upper rim of the pot to the apex of the tree, whatever its style or development. The only exceptions to this rule are the cascading and semi-cascading styles in which the tree is measured from the lower to the higher apex.

The numerous styles envisage virtually every possible type of development of the tree in the container. If we look at the Japanese styles we recognize that they can all be fitted into a triangle or series of

Classification by height:

Shito	up to 3 in (7.5 cm)
Mame	3–6 in (7.5–15 cm)
Kotate Mochi	6–12 in (15–30 cm)
Chiu Bonsai	12–24 in (30–60 cm)
Dai Bonsai	24–39 in (60–100 cm) and over

Classification by number of trees in a container:

Soju	2 trees
Samon Yose	3 trees
Gohon Yose	5 trees
Nanahon Yose	7 trees
Kyohon Yose	9 trees
Yose-ue	more than 9 trees

Classification by number of trunks on the same tree:

Tankan	1-trunk
Sokan	2-trunk
Sankan	3-trunk
Gokan	5-trunk
Nanakan	7-trunk
Kyukan	9-trunk

triangles. In practice I have always maintained that a tree manages to be convincingly beautiful only when it conforms to this geometrical shape. The rules of bonsai – the quest for the triangular form and an odd number (except for the twin-trunk style) of trunks or plants in a pot – show an interesting affinity with the beliefs of the pythagorean Greeks, back in the sixth century B.C. that the triangle was a sacred figure and that odd numbers were associated with perfection.

There are five principal styles, even though others may justifiably be considered such. In the following list the Japanese names and their English equivalents are given.

CHOKKAN
Formal upright

This consists of a single upright plant with the apex perpendicular to the base of the trunk. The branches, balanced in threes (left-back-right or right-back-left) alternate symmetrically along the trunk and thin out towards the top. The first branch, which should be about one third of the total height, determines the position of the plant in the pot, placed on the side opposite to that in which this branch is pointing.

MOYOGI
Informal upright

Although not originally accepted by purists as a true and proper style, it has become increasingly popular, not only because there are numerous examples of it in nature but also because it allows greater freedom and less blind obedience to the rules, inasmuch as it combines the features of various styles. The apex is perpendicular to the base, as in the Chokkan style, but differs in the development of the trunk, which zigzags gently upwards. The branches stem from the outside of the curves and bend slightly downwards.

SHAKAN
Slanting

The trunk is leaning, with the apex inclined at an angle of 45° to the base. The aerial development and surface roots follow the line of the trunk; the first branch, however, grows in the opposite direction, balancing the plant. This branch, which should be positioned about one third of the way up the tree, is the important determining factor in the harmonious achievement of this style.

HAN KENGAI
Semi-cascade

The tree is planted opposite to the side over which it hangs down. The style provides for two apices, one on top, situated roughly above the bend in the main branch, the other below, at the limit of plant growth. The lower apex should never exceed the height of the pot. Sometimes vegetation is only present towards the end of the trunk, which in this instance is of prime importance.

KENGAI
Cascade

Similar to Han kengai, this style differs in that the apex exceeds the height of the pot. The foliage can also grow completely outside the container, on the side opposite the base of the trunk, without touching the rim. The container has to be very tall and its choice is the determining factor in the composition's final effect.

HOKIDACHI
Broom

A few main branches arranged in a ring around the trunk support a mass of thinner branches which form a dense oval or rounded crown immediately above the base of the trunk. The tree is positioned slightly off-center in the pot, which is as a rule quite shallow. This style, frequently used in Japan with Zelkova, more or less resembles the majority of trees seen in the European countryside.

FUKINAGASHI
Windswept

A few large exposed roots follow and extend the line of the trunk, while others, generally thinner, stem from them: the tree appears to be suspended and the total effect is of airy lightness. The style is seldom used today but was at one time very popular.

This dramatically represents a tree shaped by the wind, leaning over at 45° or more. For this reason the aerial development is positioned inside the inclined part, while *jin* elements may be present on the opposite side and at the apex. It is the only style that allows branches, following the direction of the wind, to cross the trunk. The tree is planted, in a fairly shallow pot, on the side opposite to the direction of incline.

NEAGARI
Exposed roots

A few large exposed roots follow and extend the line of the trunk, while others, generally thinner, stem from them: the tree appears to be suspended and the total effect is of airy lightness. The style is seldom used today but was at one time very popular.

BUNJIN
Literati style

Simple and elegant, this style is said to have been inspired by ancient Chinese paintings which depicted trees silhouetted against the sky high in the mountains. The singular feature of the style is the disproportionately long trunk contained in a small circular or oval pot. The single slender trunk bears several thin branches, most of which are concentrated towards the apex.

BANKAN
Coiled

This style was once widespread, but is now rare, although there are some very old specimens in Japan collected from the wild. The trunk forms one or more curves that coil in on themselves. Bonsai, especially of *Pinus parviflora*, inspired by this style, have been sold and distributed since the seventeenth century.

SHARIMIKI
Driftwood

Dry wood, suitably treated, is generally used for this style. Occasionally one or two lateral branches, linked by a thin strip of bark to the roots, are used to give the impression of a tree that has survived massive natural calamities.

IKADA BUKI
Raft

Several trunks, arranged more or less parallel, form a grove or clump, seemingly joined by a single root. Actually, the grove is fashioned from a single, one-sided tree laid horizontally in a pot. The trunk is half-covered and the branches are arranged to appear like a grove of connected trees.

NE TSURANARI
Connected roots

A clump of separate plants springing from the same root. It is similar to Ikada buki but differs in the freer arrangement of the trunks. It is generally used with plants such as elms that sucker freely from the roots.

KABUDACHI
Clump

Several trunks which stem from the same base form a single tree. This style is achieved with shrubs that have several trunks or with plants that are capable of suckering at the base of the trunk, as in *Cryptomeria* and certain species of maple.

73

TAKOZUKURI
Octopus

This is a variant of the preceding style whereby the branches, stemming from the same base, snake upwards. The same name is given to a plant in which the branches wind downwards, and in either case it is derived from the evident resemblance of the branches to the tentacles of an octopus.

SEKIJOJU
Root over rock

Thick roots coil around a rock before being buried in the ground. In this style, the shape of the rock, the surface roots, and the container are as important as the shape of the plant in making a harmonious whole. Sometimes the overall effect is provided by the form and color of the rock or by the impressive structure of the roots.

ISHITSUKI
Clinging to a rock

The tree is planted directly into a rock cavity. In this style, too, the shape of the stone is extremely important, as is the moss and the presence of smaller plants which constitute a tiny fragment of the natural scene. Sometimes, to simulate an island, Ishitsuki is placed in a very low tray full of water.

SAIKEI
Tray landscape

Clearly inspired by miniature gardens of very ancient origin, this style was created by the Japanese master Toshio Kawamoto and became popular during the Second World War. It consists of a landscape in a container, formed of rocks, trees, plants, mosses, and sand to simulate a river or the sea.

NEJIKAN
Twisted

Nature offers us rare examples of this style, in which the bark alone spirals up from the base to the apex, leaving some underlying wood uncovered. The term may also describe a tree such as the pomegranate – whose trunk is twisted like cord.

Abies → entry 1
Picea → entries 68 • 69 • 70
Acacia → entry 2

ABIES/PICEA
Pinaceae

Firs and spruce – majestic trees which in their serried ranks seem to lay siege to the highest mountain peaks – have a wide distribution over the forests of the northern hemisphere. Although similar to one another, they can easily be distinguished by certain characteristics: whereas in firs the needles, generally flattened, are sessile, fixed directly to the branch and joined to it by a broad circular base, those of spruce stem separately from a persistent woody base. Firs have erect cones which flake off to release the seeds, whereas spruce have drooping cones which open when ripe. There are some 80 species of the two genera, equally subdivided. As regards their geographical distribution, it is interesting to note that in areas, sometimes quite restricted, around the Mediterranean and in Asia Minor, small species or geographical races of fir, true relicts of the last Ice Age, which ended 10,000 years ago, still thrive. At least half the species of spruce, on the other hand, originated in China. The majority of these trees have straight trunks and a conical shape, with fairly slender and flexible primary branches which bend under the weight of snow.

Abies/Picea bonsai
Few species of fir are grown as bonsai. Spruce is much more frequently used, notably *P. glehnii* and *P. jezoensis* in Japan, *P. glauca* in the United States, and *P. abies* in Europe.

ACACIA
Leguminosae

The genus contains about 1200 species of trees or shrubs, distributed for the most part in tropical and subtropical zones where they are cultivated for ornamental purposes, for their wood, and for numerous other products such as dyes, gum arabic, tannin, and perfumes. In some zones they take on a distinctive appearance at maturity: no low branches and an almost flat, spreading crown. Acacias are generally thorny plants with compound leaves, usually persistent; some Australian species have leaves transformed into phyllodes (flattened petioles) which perform the same function. They bear spikes of brightly colored flowers and flat fruits which are jointed when ripe.

Acacia bonsai
Acacias are used as bonsai especially in their countries of origin. Only a few specimens come onto the market.

Acer platanoides

ACER
Aceraceae

The genus, composed of some 150 species and innumerable cultivars, is typically found in temperate zones of the northern hemisphere, although some species grow wild on the mountainsides of Indonesia and Burma. The various species of maple differ strikingly from one another in habit, color of the trunk, type of wood, and leaves. Classification is complicated by the fact that maples hybridize readily in the wild. Whereas the few European species and the more numerous American species are for the most part of average height, the oriental maples are small trees graced by leaves that sometimes resemble natural tracery. Maples have opposite leaves, usually lobate, unisexual or bisexual flowers, and seeds contained in samaras. Many find pride of place in a garden. From certain species, particularly *Acer saccharum*, the sweet sap is extracted for use in the food industry. It is, in fact, the copious presence of sugars, typical of the species, which is responsible, among other factors, for the extraordinary coloration of the trees in autumn.

Acer bonsai
Maples are certainly very popular and widely cultivated. Perhaps the best-known species is *Acer buergerianum*, the trident maple. Splendid specimens of Japanese origin – with impressive trunk bases or roots on rock – are to be found in important collections. They are bought and sold freely in Japan and in the West.

AESCULUS
Hippocastanaceae

The genus comprises about 15 species originally from North America, southern Europe, the Himalayas, China, and Japan. Horse chestnuts are deciduous trees or shrubs with opposite leaves and white, yellow, cream or pinkish flowers arranged in showy terminal racemes up to 12 in (30 cm) long. One or more seeds are contained in a round, smooth or prickly, capsule-like involucre.

Aesculus bonsai
It is fairly common in Europe, but less so on other continents. The species *Aesculus hippocastanum* is used, and there are specimens raised from seed which are notable for their rapid growth rate and small leaves.

Aesculus pavia

79

ALNUS
Betulaceae

Known to the Romans 2000 years ago, this is a small genus of trees or, more rarely, shrubs, comprising about 35 species, mainly growing in the northern hemisphere. Alders are exceptionally well adapted to growing in wet soils near lakes and river banks. The wood has the unusual characteristic of hardening in contact with water and of being particularly resistant to it (which explains why it has been used since early times for the construction of piles, providing the foundation, incidentally, for much of the city of Venice). The leaves are deciduous, petiolate, alternate, and usually rounded, often sticky when young. The flowers are unisexual, the males arranged in drooping catkins, which appear before the leaves, and the females in oval cones, similar to small pine cones.

Alnus bonsai
Little known or used outside Europe, the alder deserves fuller attention both for its adaptability and its suitability for pruning.

ARBUTUS
Ericaceae

This genus of evergreens, known as strawberry trees, is composed of a few species: *A. unedo* and *A. andrachne*, typical of the Mediterranean flora, and *A. menziesii*, *A. texana*, and *A. arizonica* from North America. Dimensions vary, even within the same species, from that of a shrub to a tree. The simple, leathery leaves are dark green, the white or pinkish flowers, shaped like small urns, are in drooping clusters. The round fruits, with a yellowish pulp, are red or orange, edible but not very tasty, while one species, *A. unedo* derives its name from the Latin *unum edo* ("I eat only one").

Arbutus bonsai
There are a few examples of bonsai from the species *A. unedo*; it merits more attention because it adapts well to pot cultivation.

Alnus glutinosa   Arbutus unedo

BETULA
Betulaceae

Birch are true pioneering plants, and most of the 60 or so species of *Betula* are distributed over high latitudes where they flourish in extreme conditions. The deciduous oval leaves are pointed and toothed, turning bright yellow in autumn. Catkins of male and female flowers are both present on the same tree, the former appearing in autumn although they only mature in spring. The fruit is a winged, tiny nut.

White or silver birch are characteristic of northern landscapes, but the bark of some species, instead of being white, may be pinkish, yellowish pink or brown, and as a rule silky or scaly in appearance. The trees, so essential to life in northern climates, were used for making canoes, clothing, etc. Today they are widely planted in parks and gardens. They also have medicinal uses.

Betula bonsai
High adaptability, colors of the bark and of the autumn leaves, and suitability to pruning make them marvelous subjects for bonsai, especially clumps. Not particularly widespread, the genus merits more consideration.

BOUGAINVILLEA
Nyctaginaceae

The navigator Louis Antoine de Bougainville (1729–1811) gave his name to this genus, originally from tropical and subtropical America, made up of some 14 species of thorny, climbing or creeping shrubs. The leaves are entire and alternate and the small flowers would go quite unnoticed were it not for the fact that they arise from marvelously-colored, showy bracts running from red, violet, and orange to yellow and white. They are grown in the open for ornamental purposes even in zones with a warm temperate climate, for they flower in spectacular fashion for many months.

Bougainvillea bonsai
This popular plant is cultivated in many tropical lands, often far from its original range, and in temperate countries where it is treated as a house plant. In the latter instance, however, it only flowers with difficulty.

Betula pubescens

BUXUS
Buxaceae

The genus contains about 35 species found in temperate regions. Box usually takes the form of a shrub or, more rarely, a small tree, with opposite, waxy evergreen leaves, dark green above and lighter green underneath. The flowers are small, with no petals, and followed by seeds contained in a small oval capsule.

Box has for centuries been cultivated in the garden, most often to form hedges. The very hard wood is used in cabinet-making.

Buxus bonsai
The various species of *Buxus* are widely used as bonsai in Europe, the United States, and China, but less frequently in Japan.

CAMELLIA
Theaceae

The genus, composed of about 82 species originally from tropical and subtropical Asia, is named after the Moravian Jesuit, Georg Josef Kamel (1661–1706). Cultivation of camellias was nevertheless known and had been practiced in China for more than 1000 years previously.

These evergreen trees or shrubs have oval, alternate, simple, toothed, shiny, leathery leaves, showy bisexual flowers, and large, oily seeds contained in a woody capsule.

In the nineteenth century camellias generated great horticultural interest in the West and innumerable cultivars were created in a vast range of colors, from white to red with colored borders, stripes, and splashes.

The genus also includes tea-producing plants and therefore has considerable commercial importance.

Camellia bonsai
Widely known and used as bonsai, particularly in Japan, it is a very beautiful plant, the deep green leaves making a striking contrast to the smooth gray-brown bark of the trunk. It is not often seen on the market.

Buxus semperivens

CARPINUS
Betulaceae

The genus, considered to be a residue of the undergrowth of ancient forests, is made up of some 25 species from Europe, central-eastern Asia, and North America. Hornbeams are trees or shrubs with deciduous, simple, toothed, alternate leaves and unisexual flowers in male and female catkins; the fruit is a small, ribbed nutlet, protected by a leafy-looking involucre. The bark, according to the species, may be smooth or scaly, gray or gray-green; in *Carpinus laxiflora* it displays dark pink vertical bands.

Fairly undemanding plants, which respond well to pruning, hornbeams are used to line avenues and form hedges. Some species produce quite valuable timber.

Carpinus bonsai
Given its characteristics, it is much used in its countries of origin. Some species are marketed, particularly in Japan.

CASTANEA
Fagaceae

There are about 12 species in this northern hemisphere genus, growing in temperate zones of southern Europe, North Africa, eastern United States, and China. The sweet chestnuts have deciduous, alternate, toothed, short-stalked leaves and small, scented yellow-green flowers, usually unisexual; the females grow at the bases of predominantly male flowers and are covered by a spiny cup. The fruit, generally edible, is a large, brown nut with a coriaceous pericarp, covered by a spiny involucre which opens when ripe.

Known since antiquity, the sweet chestnut is grown for its fruit, wood, and other products which are used in tanning skins and in medicine; in recent decades, however, cultivation has noticeably decreased due to a devastating blight in the U.S.

Castanea bonsai
Deserving greater attention, the sweet chestnut is known but used rarely in Japan and southern Europe.

Castanea sativa

CEDRUS
Pinaceae

The four species of the genus come originally from Asia Minor, North Africa, and the Himalayas, and there are many cultivars. The cedar is generally a large tree with persistent, needle-like leaves and branches arranged in layers above one another, which give it an unmistakable appearance. Unisexual, it produces erect cones – similar to those of firs – which ripen in their second year and break up on the tree. It has been used by man since antiquity for its soft, scented, resistant wood. It is said to have furnished timber for temples in the Middle East and for the ships of the Phoenicians. Today it is widespread in parks and gardens of temperate lands.

Cedrus bonsai
It is not very common but is used successfully in the United States and Europe, thanks to its good characteristics.

CELTIS
Ulmaceae

There are about 60 species of nettle-tree or hackberries found throughout the southern and northern hemispheres. The best known, *Celtis australis*, has an enormous range that comprises southern Europe, North Africa, and a good part of subtropical Asia. The leaves are deciduous, similar to those of elm, but more oblong, lanceolate, with toothed margins; the flowers can be both unisexual or bisexual, the fruits are dark-colored drupes, according to species, and the bark is moderately rough or sometimes smooth.

Celtis bonsai
The plant is found in collections in countries of origin and sometimes appears on the market; it is particularly suitable for bonsai cultivation.

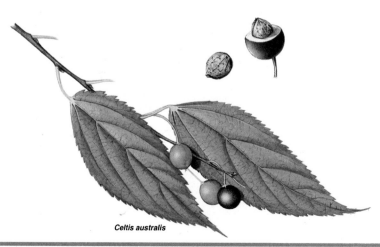

Celtis australis

Cercis → entry 21
Chaenomeles → entry 22
Cydonia → entry 29
Pseudocydonia → entry 89

CERCIS
Leguminosae

The genus contains about 6 species originally from southern Europe, North America, and Asia. The Judas tree or redbud, either a tree or a shrub, has deciduous leaves with white or violet-red, pea-like flowers which appear on the old wood and sometimes also on the trunk, before leaves emerge. The fruit is a pod containing ellipsoid seeds.

Cercis bonsai
Quite rare; a wider distribution would be desirable.

CHAENOMELES CYDONIA PSEUDOCYDONIA
Rosaceae

The genus *Chaenomeles*, formerly united with *Cydonia*, is made up of a few species only. The quince is a deciduous shrub of east Asian origin (China and Japan), with white, red, orange or pink cup-shaped flowers, followed by yellowish or reddish fruits. Widely grown for its spring flowers, it has numerous cultivars.

The genus *Cydonia* is monospecific (*C. oblonga*), although species that really belong to the genus *Chaenomeles* are often included. It is a small tree, originally from central Asia, with white or pink flowers and fruits (pomes) the size of an apple, golden yellow, and strongly scented. It is cultivated for these fruits which have various edible uses.

The genus *Pseudocydonia* is likewise monospecific. *P. sinensis*, formerly classified as *Cydonia*, is a small or large tree with semi-deciduous leaves, scaly bark, pink flowers, and large bright yellow fruits.

Chaenomeles, Cydonia, and Pseudocydonia bonsai
The genera *Chaenomeles* and *Pseudocydonia* are much used as bonsai, and there are magnificent specimens of the latter, of oriental origin.

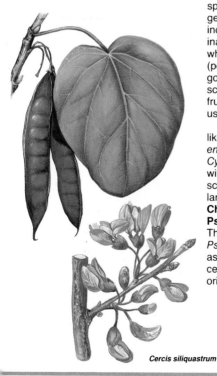

Cercis siliquastrum

CHAMAECYPARIS
Cupressaceae

Although distinct from the genus *Cupressus*, it displays some affinities to it, and it was only in 1925 that taxonomists decided to give it a separate genus. It is also interesting to note that countless cultivars have originated from three American species: the Lawson false-cypress or Port Orford cedar (*C. lawsonana*), the Nootka false-cypress (*C. nootkatensis*), and the white cedar (*C. thyoides*); and two Japanese species, the Hinoki cypress (*C. obtusa*) and the Sawara cypress (*C. pisifera*).

The *Chamaecyparis* species were at one time referred to as *Retinosporas* – mistaking Japanese trees which exhibited juvenile foliage for another genus entirely.

Chamaecyparis are evergreen, broadly pyramidal at maturity, with small scale-like leaves, male and female flowers, separated but present on the same tree, and small fruits (cones) containing winged seeds.

Chamaecyparis bonsai
Many species and cultivars are used both in the West and the Orient. Some splendid and very old specimens form part of the collection belonging to the Emperor of Japan.

CORYLUS
Betulaceae

The genus comprises 10 or so shrubby species, more rarely trees, from the northern hemisphere. The leaves of hazel are deciduous, oval, and toothed; male and female flowers are present on the same plant, the males, in drooping catkins, appearing before the leaves, the females, as small inflorescences, in spring. The fruits are oval nuts, generally edible, single or in groups, and are almost completely enclosed in an irregularly toothed, leafy bract.

Hazels are widely cultivated for their nuts or for ornamental purposes.

Corylus bonsai
Used, although rarely, in Japan and Europe.

Corylus avellana

CRATAEGUS
Rosaceae

The hawthorns are either shrubs or small trees, often with thorny branches, growing in the northern hemisphere. They have alternate, deciduous, simple, leaves, corymbs of flowers that are white to red, and fruits in the form of a pome varying from red to yellow, and sometimes edible. The genus consists of innumerable species, between 300 and 1000, according to various authors.

Crataegus bonsai
Introduced only quite recently in Japan and the West, the plant merits more attention because of its notable characteristics.

CRYPTOMERIA
Taxodiaceae
Regarded as a monotypical genus (*C. japonica*), found in China and Japan, there are many beautiful cultivars created by Japanese nurserymen. The Japanese cedar is a tree that grows to about 150 ft (45 m), with a rough reddish-brown trunk, an elongated conical habit, and a rounded apex. The needle-like persistent leaves are arranged spirally around the twigs, male and female flowers are present on the same tree, and the round terminal cones, on upward-turned stalks, are initially green and then dark brown when ripe. Several hybrids exist, including many dwarf forms.

Cryptomeria bonsai
There are many astonishing varieties, particularly in Japan. The species is also marketed. The numerous cultivars offer splendid material for bonsai and mame bonsai.

CUPRESSUS
Cupressaceae

The genus comprises some 13 species, ranging from the southern United States to Mexico and from the Mediterranean to China (the most famous being *C. sempervirens*, mentioned in the Bible and characteristic of the Mediterranean landscape). Cypresses are so enveloped in foliage that they give the impression of having no branches; indeed, despite marked differences in habit among the various species, they all display very compact growth. The trees are highly resinous and give out a characteristically strong scent, which varies from one species to another.

The twigs are covered by tiny scale-like leaves. Male and female cones appear on the same plant.

Cupressus bonsai
Used only in the United States and Europe. There are a number of old specimens collected from the wild. Young plants are particularly suitable for creating clumps.

Cycas → entry 28
Dianthus → entry 30
Diospyros → entry 31

CYCAS
Cycadaceae

The genus consists of about 20 species distributed from Madagascar to Australia. *Cycas* species are among the most ancient seed plants, with no branches, and terminal tufts of leaves. In countries with a mild climate they are also grown as ornamental subjects.

Cycas bonsai
They are cultivated in the Far East for their tropical appearance and, thanks to the expansion of the bonsai market, widely exported. One of the smallest species in the genus, and particularly prized, is *C. revoluta*. Some experts doubt whether a tree without branches can be a true bonsai, but be that as it may, its ornamental value and interest are undeniable.

DIANTHUS
Caryophyllaceae

Pinks and carnations, herbaceous annuals and perennials, make up a vast genus of about 300 species, almost all originally from temperate zones. They have long, narrow, straight, opposite leaves that come to a point. The flowers, single or in clusters, range in color from white to red, and are often scented, with two or more pairs of herbaceous bracts which form a kind of calyx. The plants are cultivated commercially for their cut flowers and scented oils.

Dianthus bonsai
In Japan the most commonly used species is *D. superbus*, in Europe, *D. deltoides*. They tend to be popular companion plants for bonsai displays and are admired for their bright summer flowers.

DIOSPYROS
Ebenaceae

A genus containing some 475 species of trees or shrubs that grow principally in tropical and warm temperate zones, persimmons have evergreen or deciduous leaves, striking bark, mostly unisexual flowers, and juicy fruit.

Some species are cultivated for their excellent wood (*D. ebenum* is the source of ebony), and others for their fruit (*D. kaki*) or for ornamental purposes (*D. lotus*).

Diospyros bonsai
In Japan *D. kaki* and *D. lotus* are both used, the former for its crop of richly colored autumn fruits.

Dianthus deltoides   **Dianthus sylvestris**

Ehretia → entry 32
Elaeagnus → entry 33

EHRETIA (CARMONA)
Boraginaceae

There are about 50 species in the genus, found in the tropical and subtropical regions of Asia and America. They are trees or shrubs with deciduous or evergreen leaves, alternate, simple or oval, dentate or entire. The flowers, normally small and white, are arranged in terminal or axillary corymbs or clusters. The fruits are red or yellow drupes, sometimes edible. They are used in their countries of origin as ornamental plants.

Ehretia (Carmona) bonsai
The best known species, *Ehretia microphylla* (*Carmona*) is cultivated in southern China and Taiwan, where there are some outstanding examples. Elsewhere the genus is little used.

ELAEAGNUS
Elaeagnaceae

There are about 60 species of oleaster, found in the temperate or warm regions of the northern hemisphere. Typically it is a small tree or shrub, sometimes thorny, with a strong root system which enables it to survive in difficult environmental conditions. The simple, stalked leaves are persistent or deciduous, bright green or silvery above, paler beneath, with tiny silver or brown hairs. The axillary flowers are single or in clusters, and the edible fruits (achenes) are covered by a fleshy red, orange-yellow or golden perianth. The genus, with its numerous cultivars, is much used in gardening.

Elaeagnus bonsai
It is used, marketed and exported from Japan, where there are some striking specimens. Elsewhere it is little used.

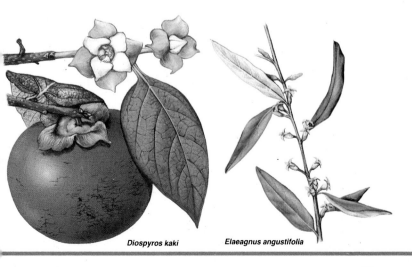

Diospyros kaki *Elaeagnus angustifolia*

EUONYMUS
Celastraceae

The genus comprises some 100 species of shrubs or small trees, mostly from eastern Asia but present almost everywhere. The spindle-trees or strawberry bushes have opposite, petiolate, usually dentate leaves; deciduous or evergreen. The young branches are quadrangular in section; the small flowers are generally bisexual and the fruits are capsules.

Various species are grown for ornamental purposes, others are used in medicine. Charcoal for drawing is obtained from the carbonized wood of *E. europaea*.

Euonymus bonsai
Some species are cultivated in Japan but rarely elsewhere.

EUPHORBIA
Euphorbiaceae

This is a vast genus of about 1000 herbaceous species, woody or cactiform, sometimes with leaves reduced to thorns. Euphorbias are characterized by cyathiform (cup-like) inflorescences, consisting of female flowers, with a long stalked terminal and central pistil, surrounded by male flowers, each reduced to a single stamen. They contain a white latex, which can be poisonous, used in medicine. The best-known species is certainly *E. pulcherrima*, known as the poinsettia.

Euphorbia bonsai
Introduction has been recent and limited to species of tree-like habit. Purists maintain that this is merely a commercial response to the demand for indoor bonsai, but they certainly provide an unusual and exotic note to any collection.

Fagus sylvatica

FAGUS
Fagaceae

There are about a dozen species of beech, found in the temperate and cold zones of Europe, Asia, and America. It is the only large tree that grows and is abundant in both hemispheres, where it often forms pure woods. It has soft, smooth or slightly rough bark, with colors that range from gray to grayish white, leaves differentiated from one species to another, and male and female flowers present on the same tree. The fruits, which appear on mature plants, are triangular achenes enclosed in a thorny capsule.

F. sylvatica, with its many cultivars, is nowadays widely used in gardens.

Fagus bonsai
F. sylvatica and *F. crenata* are the two most used species, the one in Europe, the other in Japan. The first is a hardy tree, easily taking root, with many good specimens, the second is much cultivated in the Orient and exported to the West.

FICUS
Moraceae

The huge genus contains about 600 species of trees and shrubs, some of them climbers, mostly with perennial leaves, and principally found in tropical zones. Characteristic of the genus is the milky sap and a peculiar fruit, edible in many species, called the syconium, which is actually an inverted flower.

Figs are generally used as ornamental and garden subjects, with *F. carica* widely cultivated for its edible fruit throughout the Mediterranean region. Some species, in their lands of origin, are truly monumental in appearance; others develop from the branches aerial roots which twist densely round the trunk.

Ficus bonsai
Many tropical species are used to great advantage, with stupendous buttressed trunks, spectacular exposed roots – sometimes as big as the diameter of the pot – and aerial roots which give the trees a wholly unmistakable appearance. Because they are so adaptable, they are widely sold as indoor bonsai. And in recent years even the species *F. carica* has been successfully raised.

Ficus carica

91

FRAXINUS
Oleaceae

The genus contains about 65 species of trees or shrubs with deciduous leaves, distributed mostly over the temperate regions of the northern hemisphere.

All species generally have pinnate leaves, unpaired because of the presence of a central-apical leaf, and fruits – ovoid winged samaras – containing a single seed.

F. excelsior was a tree considered by the ancient Germans to be divine, probably by reason of its height, unusual in a deciduous species – 120 ft (45 m) or more – or perhaps because the roots of the biggest specimens took over the surrounding ground, so as to form a clearing. It was also believed to have medicinal properties and was much used in herbalism.

Fraxinus bonsai
Only a few species are used, mostly in China, where they are also marketed.

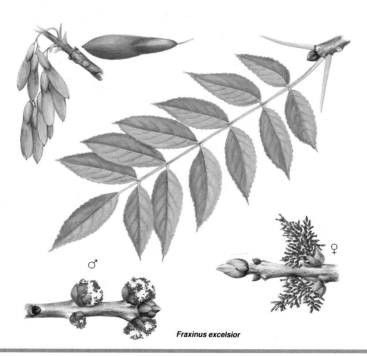

Fraxinus excelsior

GINKGO
Ginkgoaceae

The sole representative of one of the most ancient genera, the ginkgo may be considered a true living fossil (its ancestors flourished in many parts of the world during the Jurassic period, from the evidence of fossils dating back 200 million years ago, long before mankind appeared on Earth). For a long time it was believed to be extinct in its wild state and was recently rediscovered in the Chinese province of Zhejiang. Western botanists discovered it in 1727, around Buddhist temples, where it was cultivated and regarded as a sacred tree. Widely used nowadays to adorn avenues, parks, and gardens, the ginkgo displays a surprising capacity to withstand the worst conditions of pollution.

Easily distinguishable by the characteristic two-lobed, fan-shaped deciduous leaves, the tree is dioecious, with fruits appearing on female plants after about 20 years; arranged in clusters, they are hemispherical and golden yellow when ripe, after which they drop, the pulp rotting and giving out a typically sickly smell. Inside is an edible seed.

Ginkgo bonsai
It is much used, both in East and West, not only for the special form of its leaves – which turn deep yellow in autumn – but also for its great adaptability as a pot plant. Widely marketed, female plants are especially prized because they carry the fruit, but there are otherwise no morphological differences to determine the sex. The Japanese esteem those plants which exhibit characteristic projections at the base of the trunk, due to the abnormal development of the dormant shoots.

HOLARRHENA
Apocynaceae

The genus contains about 4 species of small trees or shrubs typically growing in tropical Asiatic and African zones. Among the best-known species are *H. antidysenterica*, a small Asiatian tree with bark from which is extracted various alkaloids, and seeds used by the local population to combat amoebic dysentery, and *H. africana*, which produces seeds furnished with woolly tufts which are used as padding.

Holarrhena bonsai
A little known genus. The species *H. antidysenterica* has been imported into Europe as an indoor bonsai.

Ginkgo biloba

Jacaranda → entry 47
Jasminum → entry 48
Juniperus → entries 49 • 50

JACARANDA
Bignoniaceae

These are forest plants originally from South America, usually with compound, bipinnate leaves, violet-blue or dark violet flowers and capsular fruits, sometimes edible. A fairly valuable hardwood is obtained from *J. mimosifolia*. This genus has been widely introduced and cultivated in other countries as an ornamental subject.

Jacaranda bonsai
It is used principally in tropical regions. It is found in Europe but mostly raised as a house plant.

JASMINUM
Oleaceae

There are more than 450 evergreen or deciduous species in this genus. Most are shrubs with an upright or climbing habit. Found in tropical and subtropical regions, mainly in Asia, the jasmines have ovate, trifoliolate or imparipinnate leaves, usually alternate and rarely opposite, and white, yellow or red flowers which can be pleasantly scented. Some species (*J. polyanthum* and *J. grandiflorum*) have white flowers tinged with pink on their undersides. Jasmines are widely cultivated for ornamental purposes and for the extraction of oils used in perfumery.

Jasminum bonsai
Quite often used and marketed in Japan, especially *J. nudiflorum*.

JUNIPERUS
Cupressaceae

This genus of shrubs and, less frequently, of evergreen trees, composed of some 60 species, grows mostly in temperate and cold zones. The leaves are in the form of scales or needles, and some species bear both kinds simultaneously. Sometimes dioecious, it adapts well to soil poor in humus. Ranging from the boundaries of the tropics to the Arctic polar regions, *J. communis* holds the record among trees for the most extensive range. The fruit is a cone. More than 100 cultivars and varieties are known. Classification is complicated, given the capacity to hybridize in the wild.

Juniperus bonsai
The genus, widely cultivated and marketed, is to be found in most bonsai collections. There are spectacular examples of *J. rigida* and *J. chinensis* "*Sargenti*" in Japan, and of *J. californica* in the United States.

Juniperus communis

Lagerstroemia → entry 51
Larix → entries 52 • 53
Pseudolarix → entry 90

LAGERSTROEMIA
Lythraceae

The 50 or so species of trees or shrubs belonging to this genus are from the northern and southern hemispheres. They have evergreen or deciduous, sessile, entire leaves and axillary or terminal panicles of red, pink, lavender or white flowers. The bark is smooth and sometimes flakes off.

Some species furnish good quality timber and others are cultivated successfully, outside their own range, for their beautiful flowers.

Lagerstroemia bonsai
Widely used as an ornamental plant, it is little known, indeed virtually forgotten, and quite rare in bonsai collections, but deserves better fortune.

LARIX/PSEUDOLARIX
Pinaceae

The genus contains about 10 species, with numerous subspecies and cultivars, found in the mountain and subarctic regions of the northern hemisphere. Larches are pyramidal conifers with clusters of 20–40 deciduous, acicular, jade-green leaves. They are unisexual plants, with yellow male flowers and variously colored (according to species) female flowers; the strobili are erect and persistent. Pioneer trees of great importance in forestry, larches are cultivated for their timber, much used even in high mountain zones.

Pseudolarix is a monospecific genus (*P. amabilis*), of Chinese origin. It differs from *Larix* in certain features of the male flowers and for the scales of the strobilus which fall off when ripe.

Larix/Pseudolarix bonsai
Known and valued in their original lands, they adapt well to warmer climes, especially *Pseudolarix*. They are growing in popularity.

Larix decidua

Ligustrum → entries 54 ● 55
Liquidambar → entry 56
Maba → entry 57

LIGUSTRUM
Oleaceae

The genus comprises about 50 species, found in Europe, the East and Far East. They are known as Japanese privet. They are small trees or, more frequently, shrubs, with evergreen or deciduous lanceolate leaves and panicles of white, scented flowers. The fruits, in clusters, are blackish berries. Cultivated for ornamental purposes in parks and gardens, and used to form hedges and even topiary, there are many varieties which differ from one another in coloration of leaves and in overall dimensions.

Ligustrum bonsai
Fairly well known and used in China and Japan, it is sometimes exported, but the European species are not widely distributed. It is a very lively and adaptable plant which grows fast. It deserves more widespread use.

Ligustrum lucidum

LIQUIDAMBAR
Hamamelidaceae

A genus composed of only four species, native to the warm zones of Asia and America. The trees have deciduous leaves, divided into 5–7 dentate lobes, similar to those of maple. The globose clusters of small yellow-green petalled flowers are of separate sexes but present on the same plant; the fruits are capsules.

The sweet gum is widely cultivated as an ornamental plant, even in temperate zones, for it is a vigorous grower and displays splendid autumn colors. It is also used in its native lands for its oleoresin and timber.

Liquidambar bonsai
Not one of the most commonly cultivated, it surely merits more attention.

MABA
Ebenaceae

The genus is made up of about 70 species of tropical trees or shrubs from Africa, Australia, and Asia. They have small, coriaceous leaves and round, fleshy, often edible fruits. The wood, hard and flexible, is dark in color and quite highly valued. The best known species are *M. abyssinica*, *M. natalensis*, and *M. buxifolia*. Some are cultivated elsewhere as ornamental subjects.

Maba bonsai
Little known, although there are notable specimens from Taiwan in collections in the West, where it is regarded as a house plant.

MALUS
Rosaceae

The genus is apparently made up of about 40 original species, but nobody can be certain of this because there are so many natural hybrids and cultivars; sufficient to remember that there are a thousand or so varieties of *M. domestica* alone!

The trees belonging to the genus are small or medium size, with deciduous, simple, alternate, toothed leaves. The flowers, in small corymbs, come in a vast range of colors and forms, sometimes scented, and are followed by pomes (apples) derived from the enlargement of the entire flower receptacle which becomes fleshy.

For countless centuries the apple has been widely cultivated as a fruit tree, but only around the middle of the eighteenth century did the fruits attain their present size, thanks to numerous hybridizing processes. They are also grown as ornamental subjects, particularly those varieties with an abundance of blossom.

Malus bonsai
The genus is known and used everywhere, with special emphasis on crab apples whose fruits remain on the branches after leaf fall.

MILLETTIA
Leguminosae

This genus of woody plants, similar to wisteria, composed of 90 or so species, comes mainly from Asia and tropical Africa. The leaves are compound and imparipinnate, with white, pink or reddish flowers. The seeds, sometimes edible, are contained in a large pod.

Some species furnish excellent wood.

Millettia bonsai
Certain dwarf species from Asia have recently been introduced to the market.

MORUS
Moraceae

The genus comprises only 7 species of trees or shrubs, originally from the temperate and subtropical zones of the northern hemisphere. They are monoecious or dioecious plants, with deciduous, alternate leaves, usually dentate or lobate. The flowers appear in drooping catkins, and the compound fruits are edible, and resemble elongated blackberries that are white, red or black.

Mulberries are grown even outside their original range for ornamental purposes and for their fruits. The leaves of *M. alba* are used to feed silkworms.

Morus bonsai
It is widely cultivated and marketed in Japan but high-quality specimens are few and far between.

Malus sylvestris

MURRAYA
Rutaceae

A small genus of trees or shrubs from tropical Asia and Australia. They have smooth trunks alternate, pinnate, evergreen leaves and axillary or terminal panicles of flowers. Two species, *M. paniculata* and *M. exotica*, are widely cultivated in their native lands as ornamentals, having a long flowering period and being strongly scented.

Murraya bonsai
Only *M. paniculata*, from China, is quite well known and appreciated, thanks to being widely marketed. Remarkably beautiful specimens are to be found in Oriental, European, and American collections.

MYRTUS
Myrtaceae

A genus composed of some 100 species of small evergreen trees or shrubs, growing in tropical and subtropical regions, and sometimes in temperate zones as well. Myrtles have short-stalked, aromatic, lanceolate leaves, mostly opposite, with entire margins and scented, white axillary flowers. The fruit is a berry.

The plant was sacred to Aphrodite and was used in the cult of Apollo, a symbol of happy love and of glory. The custom of making propitiatory myrtle garlands, common among Egyptian girls, was emulated by the Greeks and Romans who used them for decorating marriage feasts, and as crowns for the heads of heroes, magistrates, and poets. It is also cultivated as an ornamental and used in cabinet-making, medicine and cosmetics.

Myrtus bonsai
Used, although not so commonly, in Japan as well as Europe and elsewhere.

Olea europea

OLEA
Oleaceae

The olive was frequently mentioned in the Bible and it is certain that this plant, with thousands of years of history, in a sense signalled the dawn of western civilization. It was considered highly important by the Romans, who tried to grow it in Britain, and by the Spaniards who introduced it to the recently-conquered New World.

Probably from Asia Minor, the olive found an ideal environment in the European, Asiatic, and African lands bordering the Mediterranean. Indeed it marks off a climatic zone known as the "olive region," where the temperature seldom drops below 18°F (−8°C).

A medium-sized evergreen tree or shrub, with a spreading and often twisted base, it bears opposite, oval, leathery leaves which are glossy dark green above and silvery green below. The small flowers, in axillary clusters, are greenish white, and the fruits, drupes of varying size, are violet-black when ripe. The wood, hard, yellowish with a brown grain is widely used.

Olea bonsai
Although cultivated in many countries, only a few, principally Italy, grow and sell the olive as a bonsai. There are some remarkable specimens with stupendous bases in private collections. The species *O. oleaster* is also esteemed for its ornamental qualities and smaller leaves.

OSTRYA
Betulaceae

The genus comprises just 10 species of trees with deciduous leaves, from Asia Minor, southern Europe, and America. It is similar to *Carpinus* (hornbeam) but differs principally in the form of the fruit which is enclosed in a hairy white involucre. It is known variously as the red or black hornbeam (by reason of the reddish color of the young bark and the dark gray of the mature bark) and the hop hornbeam, after the female fruits which resemble those of the hop.

Ostrya bonsai
It is not much used outside its range.

Ostrya carpinifolia

PHILLYREA
Oleaceae

This small genus of four species is from western Asia and southern Europe, where it occupies the same range as the olive and is a constituent of the Mediterranean maquis. A tree or, more frequently, a shrub, its persistent leaves vary in shape, oval or oblong, entire or toothed, dark green above and pale green below. The short-stalked flowers, in axillary racemes, are greenish white, and the fruit is a small apiculate drupe, bluish black when ripe.

Phillyrea bonsai
Not very common, it is found in a few European collections. It deserves greater attention on the part of bonsaists.

PINUS
Pinaceae

The genus contains about 93 species, distributed for the most part over the northern hemisphere. They are evergreen trees with leaves which stem from a scaly sheath (brachyblast) and are arranged in bundles of two, three or five needles, and which may be semi-circular or triangular in cross-section. They are monoecious plants with male strobili which are red or yellow, and female strobili which are scaly and woody; the seeds are contained in a cone which ripens in the following year (except for that of *P. pinea*, which ripens after two years). The form and growth habit of the cones are generally after the number of needles.

The pines with two needles have small cones (with the exception of *P. pinea*) which are round and conical.

The pines with three needles, on the other hand, tend to have fairly large cones, also round and conical, which generally remain on the tree for several years after they ripen.

The five-needled pines mainly have cylindrical cones with soft scales. A few exceptions, such as *P. flexilis* and *P. cembra*, have woody scales and short cones.

The trees of this genus are very important in the northern hemisphere; they are grown for reforestation, for ornamental use, and for the production of edible seeds, resin, and essential oils.

Pinus bonsai
This is the best known genus and very frequently used for bonsai, both because of its evergreen appearance and its longevity. In addition to specimens in Japanese collections which are beyond praise, there are many others which are quite marvellous and very important, created from local species, often gathered from the wild. Japanese nurserymen cultivate and market *P. thunbergii* and varieties of *P. parviflora*, usually from grafts, and with particularly short needles.

PISTACIA
Anacardiaceae

The genus contains about 9 species of small trees or shrubs from the temperate or warm regions of Europe, America, and Asia. They are dioecious plants with persistent or deciduous leaves, alternate, compound, sometimes pinnate or imparipinnate. The small flowers are in axillary panicles or racemes. The fruits are drupes, usually found in clusters. Among the best-known species are the mastic trees (*P. lentiscus*), used for flavoring wines, and the pistachio (*P. vera*), which has edible nuts.

Pistacia bonsai
The Mediterranean species, meriting more attention, are little known. But there are some notable examples of the more widespread, and highly ornamental *P. chinensis*.

Pistacia lentiscus

PITHECELLOBIUM
Leguminosae

This genus of trees and shrubs comprises some 20 species, growing principally in the tropical parts of Asia and America. The leaves are bipinnate and flowers generally white or yellowish. Some species are cultivated for ornamental purposes.

Pithecellobium bonsai
Little known or used outside their original areas. Some specimens of *P. dulce* have recently been imported by dealers as house plants.

PODOCARPUS
Podocarpaceae

The genus is made up of about 94 species of coniferous trees or evergreen shrubs, distributed throughout tropical and warm temperate zones, mainly of the southern hemisphere. The leaves are linear, alternate or occasionally opposite, linear. The plants, mostly unisexual, have male flowers in cones and female flowers composed of cylindrical thickened scales. The fruits, often edible, are pedunculate, fleshy, brightly colored, drupe-like receptacles. Cultivated in their native regions both for good quality timber (Africa) and fruits (Australia), they are regarded elsewhere as ornamental subjects.

Podocarpus bonsai
The only familiar species is *P. macrophyllus*, grown in China, Japan, and the southern United States. There are specimens on the market of Chinese and, more rarely, Japanese origin.

PORTULACARIA
Portulacaceae

The genus consists of 35 species, mostly originating in warmer regions. They include herbaceous and succulent plants, sometimes shrubby, erect or prostrate in habit, with alternate leaves and panicles of bisexual flowers.

Portulacaria is made up of shrub-like succulents which sometimes grow to a height, in their native zones, of 12 ft (3 m). The shiny green leaves are thick, opposite, and obovate, the small flowers appearing on the plant when it is mature. All species are known as ornamental house plants.

Portulacaria bonsai
Used in its countries of origin, but also elsewhere, it is sometimes marketed as an indoor bonsai.

POTENTILLA
Rosaceae

The genus comprises about 500 species of herbaceous or shrubby plants from the northern hemisphere. The leaves are palmate or pinnate, the flowers white, yellow or red. Numerous hybrids exist. They are widely grown in gardens and for medicinal purposes.

Potentilla bonsai
Far removed from the classic image, this is a popular and widely marketed bonsai in Japan. It flowers for a long time during the summer, providing an attractive mass of color. The tiny trunk, with its scaly bark, creates the illusion of a miniature tree.

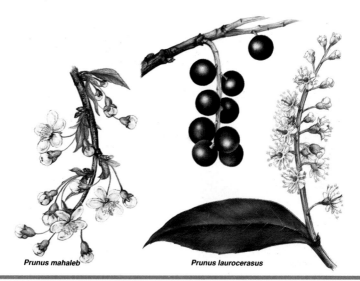

Prunus mahaleb

Prunus laurocerasus

PRUNUS
Rosaceae

About 200 species of trees or shrubs with innumerable cultivars make up this genus, most of them typical of temperate zones in the northern hemisphere. Some species (peach, cherry, plum, sloe, almond, apricot, etc.) are widely cultivated for their fruit. There are also many ornamental species, notably from the Far East, with white, pink or red sometimes scented flowers. The leaves are mostly deciduous, simple, usually with toothed margins, and they bear five-petalled flowers in pendulous or erect racemes, except for those double-flowered species which have more petals. The fruits, often edible, are one-seeded drupes.

Prunus bonsai
Well known and widely available. There are splendid specimens of *P. mume* (flowering plum) in Japanese collections.

PUNICA
Punicaceae

The genus contains only two species of trees or shrubs – *P. protopunica* and *P. granatum*. The former, originally from the island of Socotra, in the Indian Ocean, is regarded as the ancestor of the pomegranate (*P. granatum*) and is practically unknown. The latter, probably of Asiatic origin, has been widely cultivated since ancient times in the Mediterranean basin. It was already known in Egypt in 2500 B.C. and it gave its name to the Spanish city of Granada. The leaves are deciduous, opposite, pointed near the tip; the solitary coral-red flowers are bisexual, and the edible fruits are technically berries, consisting of a large number of seeds surrounded by a fleshy pulp.

The *P. granatum*, with its numerous cultivars, is found in many countries with a tropical or warm temperate climate. It grows slowly and its cultivation does not require much care, merely a sunny position. Its superb flowers make it a fine ornamental subject.

Because of its abundance of seeds, the pomegranate has become an image of fertility.

Punica bonsai
It is fairly well known in the southern United States, Europe, and Asia, where there are some excellent specimens. A dwarf variety is also used to create mame bonsai (bonsai up to 6 in (15 cm) in height).

Punica granatum

PYRACANTHA
Rosaceae

Just six species and numerous cultivars make up this genus of shrubs which come originally from southeastern Europe and central-southern Asia. Similar to *Cotoneaster*, it differs from the latter in having toothed leaves and thorns. The leaves are alternate, lanceolate, semi-permanent or persistent. The white flowers, arranged in corymbs, are followed by tiny, apple-like fruits, with a persistent calyx, which remain for some time on the plant. The fruits are brightly colored, yellow, orange or red, justifying the generic name which means ''fire thorn.'' It is widely cultivated everywhere, mainly as hedges.

Pyracantha bonsai
This bonsai is fairly popular because of its abundance of flowers, and fruits that persist all winter.

PYRUS
Rosaceae

The genus contains about 20 species of trees or, more rarely, shrubs from the northern hemisphere, and some 100 cultivars. The wild pears have deciduous, simple leaves, dentate but sometimes lobate, white flowers, often in corymbs, and rounded, typically pear-shaped fruits. Formerly the genus included *Malus*, *Aronia*, *Chaenomeles*, and *Sorbus*, but these are now separate and distinct.

Extremely tolerant with respect to soil, humidity, and temperature, the trees are widely cultivated for their fruit and more rarely for ornamental purposes.

Pyrus bonsai
Not very common, it is grown successfully in Japan and elsewhere.

Pyrus communis   **Quercus coccifera**

QUERCUS
Fagaceae

The oaks are a vast genus comprising around 600 species of trees or shrubs, including some of the most important forest trees of the temperate and subtropical zones of the northern hemisphere. They appeared on Earth about 40 million years ago and were considered by the ancient Greeks to be the first of all trees, planted by Jove; the Romans and many Nordic peoples also regarded it as sacred.

Oaks have simple, alternate leaves, deciduous or persistent, varying according to species. The plants are monoecious, with slender pendulous catkins of male flowers and spikes of sessile female flowers. The fruit is an oval or elongated acorn, partially protected by a scaly cup.

Quercus bonsai
There are few specimens of this vast and widely distributed genus in the United States and the Far East, but many excellent examples in Europe. They are very lovely trees, often with cork-like bark, and surely merit more attention.

RHODODENDRON
Ericaceae

This huge genus of trees or, more often, shrubs comprise some 850 species of azaleas and rhododendrons, mostly found in Asia.

The leaves are persistent or deciduous, simple, alternate and entire. The flowers are generally arranged in terminal, sometimes axillary, racemes, with bell- or funnel-shaped corollas. The fruit is a capsule containing many small seeds. The genus is very widely grown as an ornamental subject and has innumerable cultivars.

Rhododendron bonsai
Very well known and widely marketed, particularly in Japan. Very old and important specimens exist in all major collections.

Quercus ilex

RHUS
Anacardiaceae

A genus of about 200 species from subtropical and temperate regions. The leaves are alternate, deciduous or persistent, simple or compound; the flowers are unisexual or bisexual, and the fruits are drupes. Many species, such as *Rhus toxicodendron* (poison ivy). Some are used for ornamental purposes for the persistence of their colorful fruits in winter and many others are used industrially, thanks to the rich tannin content of the wood. The syrupy sap which serves to produce lacquer is extracted from *R. vernicifera*, cultivated in the Far East.

Rhus bonsai
Meriting more attention, it is not widely used. There are a few examples: *R. succedanea* in Japan, *R. cotinus* in Europe.

RIBES
Saxifragaceae

The genus, consisting of about 150 species, has a wide geographic distribution in the cold and temperate regions of the northern hemisphere and the Andes. The shrubs, sometimes thorny, have deciduous or persistent leaves, petiolate, alternate, simple, and lobate, and axillary flowers of various colors, both solitary and in racemes or spikes. The fruits − small round berries with a persistent calyx − vary in color according to species, and they too are single or in clusters.

The many species, cultivars and natural hybrids are grown both for ornament and for their fruit, mainly in northern Europe and North America.

Ribes bonsai
Cultivated rarely in Japan and intermittently elsewhere.

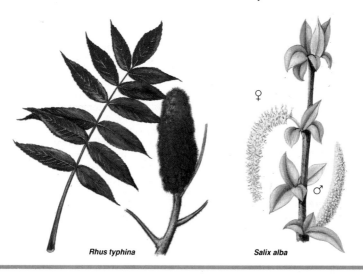

Rhus typhina

Salix alba

ROSMARINUS
Labiatae

The genus is composed of a single wild species, *R. officinalis*, typical of Mediterranean regions. It is an evergreen shrub which seldom grows taller than 5 ft (1.5 m), with narrow, opposite leaves, dark green above and greenish white below. The bisexual flowers, sometimes white but usually pale violet, justify the Latin name of the genus which means "sea dew." The stems are more or less erect, light brown, with flaking bark. Cultivated in the Mediterranean area both for ornamental purposes and to flavor foods, it is also used in medicine.

Rosmarinus bonsai
The plant is known in the U.S. and Mediterranean lands. It is particularly attractive for its long-lasting flowers and good response to pruning, and it deserves more notice.

SAGERETIA
Rhamnaceae

This genus of shrubs from tropical Asia has simple leaves, bisexual, pinkish or whitish flowers, and fruits that are drupes. The fruits of *S. brandrethiana* are edible and used in Afghanistan, while the leaves of *S. theezans* are sometimes used in China as a tea substitute.

Sageretia bonsai
Only the species *S. theezans* (= *thea*) from southern China is exported.

SALIX
Salicaceae

The genus, typical of the temperate zones of the northern hemisphere, is composed of around 300 species of trees, shrubs (sometimes of prostrate habit) and subshrubs.

The willow is a very ancient dioecious plant, dating back to the Tertiary era, some 40 million years ago. The alternate leaves, usually deciduous, take varied forms: generally they are petiolate, hairy underneath, long, narrow and pointed. The buds are unusual, covered outside by a glabrous bract, and downy inside. The unisexual flowers have no perianth and are in erect catkins. The fruit, which quickly appears, is a capsule containing fluffy seeds.

Some species are pioneer plants of high mountain regions, whereas others prefer wet zones such as river banks and lake shores. Willows are cultivated for their flexible branches, used in basketry, and weeping species are grown for ornamental use in parks and gardens. For centuries they have been known for their pain-relieving properties because of their high content of salicylic acid.

Salix bonsai
It is used, though infrequently, in Europe and America, and even more rarely in the Orient. It grows rapidly and can therefore be cultivated in a relatively short time.

Schefflera → entry 104
Scolopia → entry 105
Semiarundinaria → entry 106

SCHEFFLERA
Araliaceae

This genus of evergreen trees and shrubs is made up of about 200 species that are widely distributed in tropical regions. They have palmately-compound leaves and panicles of five- or six-petalled flowers.

Schefflera bonsai
Not very often used; in recent years, however, many examples of *S. actinophylla*, usually in rock style, have been sold as house plants.

SCOLOPIA
Flacourtiaceae

A genus of some 40 species of thorny trees or shrubs from Africa, Asia, and Australia. They have spirally arranged leaves, inconspicuous flowers in axillary racemes, and berry-like fruit.

Scolopia bonsai
It is rarely cultivated, though some specimens from China are sold from time to time.

SEMIARUNDINARIA
Gramineae

A genus comprising about 30 species of evergreen bamboos. The creeping rhizome is branched, the stems are jointed with nodes and internodes, and the leaves are lanceolate. The flowers are in panicles or racemes.

The plants are peculiar in that they usually die after flowering. Fortunately this only occurs at very long intervals, sometimes more than 100 years. Flowering, when it occurs, is generally simultaneous throughout the world within a given species.

Semiarundinaria bonsai
The genus is indigenous to Japan and very popular there, used mainly to create unusual-looking clumps. It is sometimes marketed.

Sequoia sempervirens

Sequoia → entry 107
Serissa → entry 108
Spiraea → entry 109

SEQUOIA
SEQUOIADENDRON
Taxodiaceae

The genus *Sequoia* contains only one species – a huge evergreen tree, known as the redwood, although another North American sequoia, *Sequoiadendron giganteum* (giant sequoia), was formerly included in the same genus.

The two sequoias differ in the form of the leaves – flat and acicular in *Sequoia sempervirens*, squamiform in *Sequoiadendron giganteum* – and in the size of the cones.

Redwoods and giant sequoias are monoecious. The winged seeds are contained in cones which mature in one year in *Sequoia sampervirens* and in two years in *Sequoiadendron giganteum*, on which they remain closed for about 20 years. Not very fertile, they have the peculiarity, unusual for conifers, of sprouting new growth at the base of stumps.

Pyramidal in habit, redwoods grow to an astonishing height, one specimen having grown to a record 365 ft (111 m). Another of their characteristics is longevity: some specimens of *Sequoiadendron giganteum* are more than 1,500 years old, although some authors claim the true figure is closer to 4,000 years. Older trees have bark which is some 24 in (60 cm) thick.

Sequoia bonsai
A few specimens, some of them very lovely, are grown on the west coast of the United States and in important American collections.

SERISSA
Rubiaceae

This family of dicotyledons, distributed principally in tropical regions, contains the coffee plant and the gardenia. The genus is made up of evergreen shrubs with entire, opposite leaves and small bisexual flowers, generally white.

Serissa bonsai
It owes much of its popularity to large-scale exports from China and Taiwan. In the West it is considered a house plant, particularly valued for its flowers.

SPIRAEA
Rosaceae

A genus of shrubs composed of about 80 species, from the northern hemisphere. Spiraeas have deciduous, alternate, dentate or lobate leaves, and racemes, corymbs or feathery panicles of white, pink or red flowers.

Many species are grown as ornamental subjects; some also yield an oil used occasionally in the perfume industry.

Spiraea bonsai
Several species are cultivated in Japan, particularly as mame bonsai, and widely marketed; they are less popular elsewhere.

SYRINGA
Oleaceae

The genus contains, apart from numerous cultivars and natural hybrids, about 25 species, most of them originating in south-eastern Europe and the Far East. Generally shrubs, more rarely small trees, they have decid-uous, opposite, entire leaves. The white, lilac or reddish flowers, often scented, are ar-ranged in showy terminal in-florescences.

Widely cultivated for orna-ment, they are used as cut flowers and for the production of perfume essences.

Syringa bonsai
Little known, but surely deserv-ing more attention. Examples of dwarf varieties have recently been marketed in Japan.

TAMARINDUS
Leguminosae

This genus, from tropical Asia and Africa, contains trees some-times up to 100 ft (30 m) tall, with pendulous branches, evergreen, pinnate leaves, and pendulous racemes of yellow flowers veined in red. The pods are up to 4 in (10 cm) long and contain 3–10 seeds inside a sourish juicy pulp, much used in cooking. The leaves are sometimes used as cattle fodder. In tropical coun-tries the tamarind is widely grown for ornament.

Tamarindus bonsai
Cultivated mainly in the tropics but sometimes imported as house plants.

Taxodium distichum

TAMARIX
Tamaricaceae

The genus comprises about 54 species of deciduous or evergreen shrubs, more rarely trees. Tamarisks have slender, feathery secondary branches covered with tiny sessile, squamiform leaves, and an abundance of white or pink flowers in cylindrical racemes. The yellow, hairy seeds are contained in a trigonal-pyramidal capsule.

With a vast distribution over parts of Europe, Africa, and Asia, this is one of the few genera to thrive in salty soil along the seashore. Tamarisks are grown as ornamental subjects and as windbreaks in coastal areas.

Tamarix bonsai
Cultivated both in China and Japan, it is sometimes exported, but is rare elsewhere.

TAXODIUM
Taxodiaceae

This genus, comprising only three species, has a range that extends from the southern United States to Mexico. The two North American species (*T. distichum* and *T. ascendens*) are deciduous, growing in swampy zones, sometimes submerged in the water. With age, *T. distichum*, the bald-cypress, develops special protruding roots known as pneumatophores, around the base. These are thought to supply oxygen to roots that are growing in water-logged soil. *T. mucronatum*, an evergreen, is the national tree of Mexico. Near Santa Maria de Tule there is a specimen over 2,000 years old, with a trunk circumference of almost 120 ft (35 m) – probably a world record.

The bald-cypress is a monoecious tree, with narrow, soft, flat leaves in two rows. There are male flowers in branched, pendulous clusters and rounded female cones which break up when ripe, releasing the seeds.

Taxodium bonsai
Trees of extraordinary adaptability and vigorous growth, they can be adapted as pot plants. Numerous splendid examples exist in U.S. collections, but not in those of the Orient.

Tamarix gallica

TAXUS
Taxaceae

A small genus containing only seven species but countless cultivars of evergreen trees or shrubs. Taxonomists are not in complete agreement as to the specific classification of the yews, which have very similar features, some preferring to list them as geographical races of a single species.

The yew is an extremely ancient tree, with relatives going back some 200 million years, considered sacred by the Celts and used, thanks to the resistance and flexibility of the wood, for making bows and arrows. In Germany it is called *Todesbaum* (tree of death); all parts are, in fact, poisonous, except for the aril. A dioecious tree, it has unisexual flowers present in the axils, dark green above and paler green below. The hard, woody seeds are partially covered by a juicy red aril.

With its numerous cultivars, yew is widely used as a hedge and ornamental shrub of great versatility. The plant is slow-growing and very long-lived; there are many specimens in cultivation thousands of years old.

Taxus bonsai
The best-known species, *T. cuspidata*, is used mainly in Japan, where it is marketed. Elsewhere it is little known. *Taxus baccata*, the English yew, is widely grown in Europe as an ornamental.

THYMUS
Labiatae

This genus of evergreen plants comprises about 350 species of shrubs and herbs, originally from temperate regions of Europe and Eurasia and found particularly in the Mediterranean area. The best-known species of thyme, *Thymus vulgaris*, has a twisted, woody trunk, with dense, upright branches and small, sessile, lanceolate, pubescent leaves, whitish underneath. The small pink or white flowers are in terminal spikes.

Thyme is much appreciated in cookery for its pleasant aroma and also in medicine and perfumery.

Thymus bonsai
Highly regarded for its strong fragrance and long-lasting summer flowers, thyme is used principally in Mediterranean lands for creating mame bonsai.

Taxus baccata

TILIA
Tiliaceae

The genus comprises some 45 species of trees and shrubs, found in the temperate parts of the northern hemisphere. Linden (lime) trees have deciduous, alternate, simple, petiolate leaves, and clusters of fragrant bisexual flowers borne on a membranous bract. The fruit is a capsule often adorned with a bract.

A long-lived plant, the linden has captured human imagination since antiquity and many legends concerning it date from pre-Hellenic times; it is considered in all mythologies as the essential female tree. It is used for ornament and in medicine.

Tilia bonsai
Cultivated on a small scale in Europe, the linden merits greater attention because of its adaptability and vigorous growth.

TSUGA
Pinaceae

The genus, with a range that comprises North America, the Himalayas, and the Far East, consists of 10 or so species, numerous natural hybrids and cultivars. Hemlocks have flat acicular leaves, similar to those of fir and spruce, although softer. Male and female flowers are present on the same tree at the tips of the branches, and characteristically mature at different times, so as not to be self-fertilizing. Pendulous cones bear two seeds to every scale. The trees are cultivated for ornamental purposes and as forest species.

Tsuga bonsai
Fine examples are found in Japanese and some European collections. The native species of North America are more rarely used.

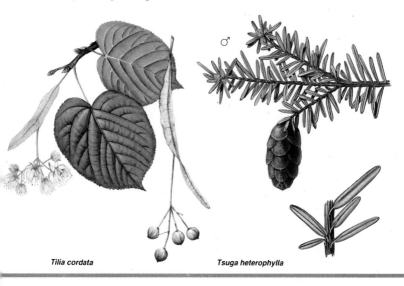

Tilia cordata

Tsuga heterophylla

ULMUS
Ulmaceae

A genus of trees or shrubs growing in the temperate zones of the northern hemisphere. According to different authors, there are from 20 to more than 40 species of elm, but some claim that there are over 200. Because elms naturally hybridize with one another, classification and identification are difficult, and the truth is that nobody really knows how many species exist.

The Ainu – a population living in the northernmost islands of the Japanese archipelago – believe that the elm was the first tree that appeared on Earth to provide fire for mankind; this belief may have originated in the fact that the dry roots, when rubbed, give out sparks.

The trees bear deciduous, rarely persistent, alternate, and dentate leaves, dense inflorescences of small, bisexual flowers and fruits in the form of winged nuts (samaras).

Ulmus bonsai

The genus is widely distributed, grown, and marketed everywhere. In China and Japan there are particularly fine specimens of *U. parviflora* and cultivars with very small leaves.

Ulmus laevis   **Ulmus glabra**

VITEX
Verbenaceae

The genus is comprised of about 250 species, mainly found in tropical and subtropical zones but also in some temperate regions. These include evergreen or deciduous trees and shrubs, characterized by pronounced polymorphism of leaves. The flowers are generally arranged in sweet-smelling clusters. Many species furnish valuable timber.

Vitex bonsai
Fairly common in southern China and Taiwan, but little known elsewhere.

WISTERIA
Leguminosae

The genus is made up of six species of climbing plants or shrubs, originally from North America and eastern Asia. Wisterias have deciduous, pinnate leaves and pendulous clusters of white, pink or violet flowers, which can be fragrant. Bloom can be in spring as the leaves appear, or in summer.

Wisteria sinensis, introduced to the West from China in 1818, is widely used as an ornamental subject.

Wisteria bonsai
Much used and freely marketed both in China and Japan. Found commonly in Europe and the U.S. Although the finest specimens do not usually have a particularly interesting structure, they are nevertheless attractive and appreciated for their extraordinary spring flowers.

ZELKOVA
Ulmaceae

A small genus comprising only five species of trees and shrubs, with a range including Japan and Crete. There are two oriental species (*Z. serrata* and *Z. sinica*), two Caucasian (*Z. carpinifolia* and *Z. verschaffeltii*) and one originally from the mountains of Crete (*Z. cretica*).

The *Zelkova* species have a smooth gray trunk, alternate, deeply toothed leaves, scabrous underneath. The fruit, a small drupe, distinguishes zelkovas from elms.

Zelkova bonsai
Much used in Japan, they have become widely known from exported specimens. The classical style in which they are cultivated in the *Hokidachi* or broom-style for which they are particularly well suited because of the many dense branches.

Zelkova carpinifolia

1 ABIES NEBRODENSIS Mattei

It belongs to one of the species or geographic races which remained trapped within a restricted zone during the last Ice Age, in this instance the Nebrodi Mountains of northern Sicily. Almost extinct in the wild, it is very similar to *Abies alba*, differing in its lesser size, its stiffer habit and shorter, denser needles.

Repotting Every 2–3 years in early spring, with 60% soil, 10% peat, and 30% coarse sand.

Pruning and wiring Major treatment of the root system should be done at the same time as the pruning of the aerial part. It is possible to shorten the branches somewhat, leaving 1–2 shoots. To thicken the foliage, pinch the new shoots while still tender, reducing them by two thirds. In spring carry out wiring to position the trunk and branches.

Feeding Once a month just before and during the growing season, stopping for a brief interval in summer, with a last application in autumn. If the temperature does not fall below freezing, it is advisable to fertilize lightly (¼ dose) in winter as well.

Notes Because as a rule the structure of the fir changes gradually when kept in a pot, it is best to acclimatize the plant in a large container before setting it in the bonsai pot.

---

2 ACACIA sp

Introduction – see p.78

Repotting Every 2–3 years in spring. Acacias are not particularly demanding as regards soil composition, but it is best to add 30% coarse sand or equivalent material.

Pruning and wiring Carry out major work on the roots during the first repotting at the same time as the foliage is reduced; prune and shape aerial part after flowering; wire from spring to autumn. Bearing in mind that the woody branches are rather delicate, proceed with caution and repeat the wiring procedure at 2-year intervals. Protect the bark and check the wiring during the growing period.

Feeding Every 15–20 days before and during the growth period, using half the dose of fertilizer recommended by the makers.

Notes These plants, which come mostly from countries with a hot climate, enjoy light and should be kept at temperatures above 50°F (10°C) or protected in a greenhouse in winter. If raised indoors, keep them in a well lit, airy place, with a temperature of not more than 64°F (18°C). Allow the soil to dry between waterings and spray the foliage once a day with water at room temperature. As soon as weather conditions permit, put the plant outdoors in direct sunlight and water regularly.

3 ACER BUERGERIANUM

Originally from China and Japan, it is notable for its fairly small, 3-lobed leaves. It is certainly the maple most often used for bonsai, because of its extreme adaptability and the potentially broad development of the base of the trunk.

Repotting The plant throws out a large number of roots and should therefore be repotted every year or two (old specimens, every 2–3 years), after the leaves fall or before they appear, with 60% soil, 20% peat, and 20% coarse sand.

Pruning and wiring Drastic root pruning should be done at the same time as repotting. In late spring shape the tree by reducing the new shoots to the first 2 leaves. Carry out positional wiring during the growth period, taking care to protect the bark. Some leaves can be removed, leaving the stalk, in late spring.

Feeding Before and during the growing season and in early autumn, every 3 weeks, with an interval in midsummer.

Notes The soil should never dry out completely, so protect from direct sun in summer and frost in winter. The branches are rather fragile, so take care with wiring. Given a thick trunk base and strong lateral roots, eliminate the tap-root or roots lying directly beneath the base.

4 ACER CAMPESTRE L.

Distributed in Europe, North Africa, Asia Minor, the Caucasus, and northern Iran, this is a hardy plant which lends itself well to pot cultivation. It has 3–5 lobed leaves and gray-brown bark, fissured when mature. It is distinguished from other species of maple by the leaves which have obtuse lobes, the central one often trilobate.

Repotting With its vigorous growth, the plant should be repotted at least once every 2 years, in early spring or late autumn, with 70% soil, 10% peat, and 20% coarse sand.

Pruning and wiring Pruning of the roots should be carried out at the same time as repotting and positioning of the aerial part. Scars will form quickly and well if a special compound is applied. Wiring and positioning of branches should be done in late spring and probably repeated at yearly intervals, given that the bigger branches are rather stiff.

Feeding From early to late spring and late summer to early autumn, every 20–30 days.

Notes To reduce the overall size of the leaves, cut off the largest in early or mid June, leaving the stalks. When new leaves appear, water sparingly. The plant may be kept in full sun (which is unusual for maples) but needs to be watched so that the soil does not dry out completely.

5 ACER MONSPESSULANUM L.

A small tree or shrub from southern Europe, northwest Africa, and Asia Minor. The leaves – smaller than those of all other maples in this range – are 3-lobed with an obtuse tip, paler below than on top. The bark of the trunk, pale gray, is rough when mature.

Repotting Every 2–3 years during spring or autumn, with 70% soil and 30% coarse sand or equivalent material.

Pruning and wiring The first major pruning of the roots should be at the same time as repotting and selective trimming of the aerial part. In late spring cut back the shoots to 2–4 leaves. Repeat the operation during the growing season. Wiring can be done from spring to autumn, taking care because the bigger branches are rather delicate. The bark, too, must be protected.

Feeding Once every 20–30 days from early spring to autumn, stopping for about a month in midsummer.

Notes The plant relishes sun and dry conditions. These characteristics, unusual in the genus, can be exploited in order to obtain small leaves and short internodes by keeping the plant well exposed to sunlight and watering only when the soil is partially dry.

6 ACER PALMATUM Thunb.

This species of maple, originally from China and Japan, is notable for its leaves with 5 (sometimes more) lobes and pointed tip. It is one of the most popular bonsai in Japan. The bark of the trunk, usually green when young, may turn brown or gray-white with age.

Repotting Every 2 years in spring, when the buds swell prior to opening, or in autumn after leaf fall; 60% soil, 20% peat, and 20% coarse sand.

Pruning and wiring The first pruning of the root system should be carried out only at the time the aerial part is reduced. It is best to do the repotting and pruning in autumn so as to avoid excess loss of sap as maple wounds tend to "bleed" heavily when the sap rises in spring. Seal wounds with a special compound. Attend to wiring in spring, remembering that the bark is rather thin and the branches none too elastic; protect the branches and trunk, positioning them gradually with care.

Feeding Every 20–30 days from spring to autumn, with an interval in midsummer.

Notes In the growing season shorten the new shoots, leaving the first 2 leaves. Defoliation is possible in early summer. Avoid exposure to direct sunlight in hot weather; water generously early morning or late afternoon to prevent soil from drying out.

7 ACER PSEUDOPLATANUS L.

A medium-sized tree with a fairly long life, growing over a vast area from the Pyrenees to the Caucasus, mainly in mountain woodland and widely planted as a street tree in the U.S. The simple leaves are quite large, 4–6 in (10–15 cm), with long stalks, 5-pointed and toothed lobes, dark green above and blue-green below.

Repotting Every 2–3 years in autumn or spring, with 70% soil, 20% coarse sand or equivalent material, and 10% peat.

Pruning and wiring The first pruning and positioning of the roots should coincide with repotting and the selective reduction of the aerial part; wire to shape the trunk and branches from spring to autumn.

Feeding Every 20–30 days stopping for about one month in midsummer.

Notes The soil should not dry out entirely; keep in a well-lit place but avoid prolonged exposure to the sun in summer. This is one of the few plants in which leaf removal is essential, because of their large size, and they should be cut back to half the length of the stalk in the early summer, once leaves have fully expanded and thickened. This operation should only be carried out if the plant is healthy and well fed. Water sparingly as new shoots emerge.

8 AESCULUS HIPPOCASTANUM L.

The horse-chestnut comes from eastern Europe and the Caucasus, with opposite, long-stalked, compound leaves, toothed at the margins and pointed at the tip.

Repotting Every 2–3 years in early spring or autumn, with 80% soil, rich with humus, and 20% coarse sand.

Pruning and wiring Reduction or elimination of the tap-root should coincide with repotting and only if there are strong lateral roots. Limit pruning of branches to a minimum, bearing in mind that the horse-chestnut does not easily form scar tissue. Shape the tree mainly by trimming the shoots, removing the apical shoots during winter dormancy. To stimulate the growth of new leaves, eliminate the bigger ones, cutting back to a third of the stalk length. Carry out wiring from spring to summer.

Feeding Every 15–20 days at start of and during growth period, stopping for about a month in midsummer.

Notes This is one of the few plants which should be grown from seed, both to encourage strong growth – which will produce a good specimen within a few years – and also to avoid ugly scars. Sow in autumn in a shallow pot with 50% soil and 50% sand. Transplant the following year, shortening the tip and reducing the tap-root. Proceed as described above during the growing period.

9 ALNUS CORDATA Loisel.

The Italian alder is a fairly large tree with a slender, straight trunk, the bark gray-green with whitish streaks, fissured when mature. The leaves are simple, alternate, petiolate, cordate, finely serrate with a pointed tip. It comes from the central-southern Mediterranean region, including southwestern Italy, Sicily, Corsica, and Sardina.

Repotting Early spring or autumn, every 2–3 years, with 70% soil, 20% coarse sand, and 10% peat.

Pruning and rewiring Late autumn or winter. Major work on the root system should be done gradually, especially with old plants. The branches, too, can be shortened during the winter, preferably leaving a few buds. Shorten the new shoots in the growing season when they are still tender, retaining a pair of leaves. Wire in spring, taking care to protect the trunk and branches.

Feeding Once every 20–30 days, at the beginning of and during the growth period.

Notes The plant is a strong grower and particularly likes humidity. Avoid letting the soil dry out completely but also avoid standing water. When the plant is in a bonsai container it is advisable not to expose it to direct sun during the summer.

---

10 ARBUTUS UNEDO L.

The strawberry tree is a typical constituent of the Mediterranean flora, with simple, alternate, persistent, leathery, serrate leaves, and reddish-brown trunk and branches with bark that flakes off in thin strips at maturity.

Repotting Every 2–3 years in early spring. Exceptionally for the Ericaceae, it tolerates the presence of lime. It is best to use 70% soil and 30% coarse sand or equivalent material.

Pruning and wiring Because the plant is an evergreen with flowers and fruits throughout the year, it is advisable to get rid of these at first repotting. If initial pruning of the roots is sufficiently drastic, the leaves may be completely removed. Prune the tree during growth, shortening new shoots to the first 2–3 leaves. Carry out wiring from spring to autumn, protecting the trunk and branches.

Feeding Every 20–30 days from early spring to autumn, with a short interval in midsummer.

Notes Although garden specimens can withstand temperatures around 32°F (0°C), when the plant is in a bonsai pot the root system needs protection from frost. It reacts well to wiring, thanks to its flexible wood, but shortage of water may cause the leaves to lose stiffness.

11 BETULA VERRUCOSA Ehrh.

The European white birch has a vast range that comprises most of Europe except for Spain and Portugal. In the south it grows principally in the mountains, but in the north, and even at very high latitudes, it is found in lowland areas.

Repotting In early spring every 2–3 years, with 60% soil, 20% peat, and 20% coarse sand.

Pruning and wiring Prune the root system at the same time as the aerial part is reduced, while positioning the plant. Shape by pruning, during early winter, and keep growth under control by shortening new shoots before they lignify, to 2–4 leaves. Wiring should be done while the plant is growing, taking care to protect the trunk and branches.

Feeding After the leaves show and during the entire growing period, stopping about a month in midsummer. In late summer and autumn use a complete fertilizer high in potassium.

Notes The birch needs light and water; never allow the soil to dry out and provide shade in low latitudes and warmer climate zones. Since the thin, peeling white bark is one of the most attractive features of the European white birch, it is essential not to damage it when wiring. Also check the wires frequently during the growing season to make sure they are not digging into the bark. Remove suckers which arise from the base of the trunk promptly.

---

12 BOUGAINVILLEA GLABRA Choisy

An evergreen plant, originally from South America, which may be transformed into a deciduous species in less favorable climates, without ill effect.

Repotting Every 2–3 years in early spring, with 70% soil and 30% coarse sand.

Pruning and wiring Do not prune the root system too severely; just shorten the tap-root and the bigger roots after flowering or during repotting. Repeat the operation the following year. Pruning to shape the crown can be done at any time of year, although preferably after flowering or long before it. When trimming new shoots, bear in mind that the flowers of bougainvillea sprout from the tips. Therefore, a decision must be made whether to encourage flower production or to have denser foliage. Wire during the growth period.

Feeding Repeat at two-week intervals while in flower, once a month from spring to late summer.

Notes Although bougainvillea adapts easily to its surroundings, it has to be protected against freezing temperatures. Water frequently while flowering, but after this only if the soil dries out completely. It grows well in the sun, but if you move it from the shade into a sunny position, gradually increase exposure to direct sunlight to avoid the leaves burning. It will also thrive in a sunny position indoors.

13 BUXUS HARLANDII Hance

This species, originally from China, is known internationally through bonsai. The foliage is dense with small leaves, the trunk is a fairly pale yellowish brown, and the bark is fissured and cork-like. The plant is slow-growing.

Repotting Every 2–3 years in spring, with 60% soil, 30% coarse sand, and 10% peat. It appreciates some ground limestone.

Pruning and wiring Pruning of the roots should be effected in spring at the same time as the first repotting and the reduction of aerial part. Standard pruning is carried out during growth by reducing new shoots to 2–4 leaves. Wiring may be done at any time of year.

Feeding From spring to autumn, every 20–30 days.

Notes Allow the soil to dry out between waterings. Box is an adaptable plant which can withstand many shocks that may result from sudden changes of environment. Avoid direct exposure to sunlight in summer and protect in a greenhouse in winter. Indoors it should be placed in bright and not excessively warm positions; if the temperature goes above 65°F (18°C), spray the foliage once or twice a day and feed sparingly (¼ dose every 20 days) even during the winter.

---

14 CAMELLIA JAPONICA L.

The plant comes from southern Japan, Korea, and China.

Repotting Every 2–3 years in early spring and after flowering, with 60% acidic and humus-rich soil, 20% peat, and 20% coarse sand.

Pruning and wiring The first pruning of the root system should coincide with the trimming of the foliage. Because camellias have fairly superficial roots, drastic treatment is seldom needed; proceed gradually and repeat light pruning the following year. On plants that are in training, prune the aerial part in the growing season, as and when necessary, while on those that are already formed it is advisable to cut back the foliage right after flowering. Wiring can be done from late spring to autumn: protect the branches and trunk and proceed very carefully because of their fragility.

Feeding From spring to autumn, every 15–20 days, with fertilizers formulated for acid-loving plants.

Notes The soil should not be allowed to dry out completely, even in winter. Protect the plant under glass in winter and from excessive heat and temperature fluctuations in summer.

15 CARPINUS BETULUS L.

The hornbeam is a medium-sized tree, ranging from central-southern Europe to western Asia. The bark is ash gray, and the short-stalked leaves are alternate, doubly dentate, with a pointed tip, paler underneath. The fruits are achene-like nutlets, protected by a trilobate bract with an elongated central lobe.

Repotting Every 2–3 years in early spring. The plant is not particularly demanding, and 70% soil and 30% coarse sand will suffice.

Pruning and wiring Initial pruning of the roots should coincide with the first repotting and reduction of the aerial part. The hornbeam withstands and responds well to repeated pruning, quickly forming scar tissue. Wiring to shape the trunk and branches can be done from spring to autumn, taking care to protect the bark.

Feeding Once a month from early spring to autumn, stopping for 30–40 days during the heat of midsummer.

Notes An ideal plant without particular needs. It thrives in sun but should be kept in partial shade in summer. Never let the soil become completely dry, and rub off undesirable suckers from trunk and roots. When pruning the tree to shape, it is important to remember that the new growth will follow in the direction of the shoot that remains directly behind the cut.

16 CARPINUS LAXIFLORA Bl.

A small tree originally from the temperate zones of Japan, characterized in nature by the drooping habit of the branches and the elliptic, prominently-veined leaves with pointed tip.

Repotting In early spring, generally once every 2 years, or if the pot is fairly small, every year: 60% soil, 20% peat, and 20% coarse sand.

Pruning and wiring The first drastic pruning of the roots should be done at the same time as repotting but only if the root system is strong. If not, shorten the tap-root and the thicker roots, and repeat the operation in successive years. If the plant is already growing in a pot, simply remove the roots that have formed directly above the drainage holes or around the container, and then shorten the tap-root and bigger roots. In spring trim the foliage to shape, reducing the new shoots to the first 2 leaves. Wiring can be done at the same time.

Feeding Every 20–30 days from early spring to autumn, with a gap in midsummer.

Notes Since this is a plant with strong apical growth, it is necessary to resort to drastic pruning of the upper part of the tree, while cutting back the lower part conservatively. The soil should never be allowed to dry out completely. Expose to full sun in winter, spring, and autumn; semi-shade in summer.

17 **CASTANEA SATIVA** Miller

The sweet chestnut is a tree of medium size and great longevity, with dark brown bark which is initially smooth and later rough. The original range is unknown, given the wide cultivation of this species since remote times. Today it is found growing wild from the Iberian peninsula to the Caucasus.

Repotting Every 2–3 years in autumn or early spring. It prefers acidic soil (60%) with the addition of 20% peat and 20% coarse sand or equivalent material.

Pruning and wiring Pruning of the root system should coincide with repotting and reduction of aerial part. Shorten the shoots to the first 2 leaves during the growing season. Carry out wiring in spring–summer, protecting the bark of the bigger branches and the trunk.

Feeding Every 20–30 days from early spring to autumn, stopping for a month in midsummer.

Notes The plant is a strong grower without particular problems, but it has the defect, for a bonsai, of having rather large leaves. So one should choose medium–tall specimens in order to have a better proportion of trunk to foliage. Because the tree tends to lose leaves which are left in shade inside the branches, it is advisable to eliminate the bigger leaves and ensure that all parts of the plant are well exposed to the light. The soil must never be left completely dry.

18 **CEDRUS LIBANI** A. Rich

The cedar of Lebanon is a tree of medium size originally from Asia Minor, and is widely cultivated for ornamental purposes. The trunk is dark gray, smooth when young, fissured with age.

Repotting Every 3–5 years in spring or end of summer–beginning of autumn. Use 70% soil, 20% coarse sand, and 10% peat.

Pruning and wiring Initial work on the roots should be carried out at the time of the first repotting and selective pruning of the aerial part. Reduce the root system gradually. To thicken the foliage, pinch the still tender new shoots with the nails, cutting back the length by two thirds. Wiring may be done at any time, but should be left for at least 3 months after repotting.

Feeding Once a month at the beginning of and during growth.

Notes The plant likes mild temperatures and sun and should therefore be protected in winter. To encourage rooting after repotting and to keep it healthy in the summer, spray the foliage at least once daily. Water abundantly only when the soil is partially dry.

19 CELTIS AUSTRALIS L.

Of medium size, the southern nettle-tree is distinguished from other species by its toothed leaves with pointed tip, downy underneath, and its dark red fruits.

Repotting Every 2–3 years in early spring or autumn, with 70% soil and 30% coarse sand or equivalent material.

Pruning and wiring Carry out the first drastic pruning to position the root system when repotting. If there are no good lateral roots to guarantee success, repeat the operation every 2 years. Trim the aerial part from late spring to early autumn, reducing the new shoots to the first 2 leaves. Shape by wiring the trunk and branches in the growing season, taking care to protect the bark.

Feeding Every 20–25 days at the start of and during the growth period, stopping for about a month in midsummer.

Notes The plant poses no special problems, responds well to drastic pruning and forms scar tissue easily. Keep in a well-lit position, avoiding direct and prolonged exposure to the sun during the hottest part of summer. Water only when soil is partly dried out. Protect, especially the roots, in prolonged frosts.

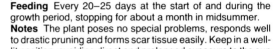

20 CELTIS SINENSIS Pers.

Originally from the Far East – China, Japan, and Korea – this Chinese nettle has dark green leaves, almost shiny on the upper side, and drupes that are red or yellow in some varieties.

Repotting Every 1–2 years in early spring, with 70% soil and 30% coarse sand or equivalent material.

Pruning and wiring If the lateral roots are strong, the root system can stand drastic pruning at the same time as repotting and reduction of aerial part. Although it forms good scar tissue, it is necessary to protect the bigger wounds with a sealer. Prune foliage to shape during growth period by shortening the new shoots to the first 2–3 leaves. At the same time, position the trunk and branches with wire, protecting the bark.

Feeding Apply plentifully every 25–30 days from early spring to autumn, with a gap of about one month in midsummer.

Notes An easy plant to cultivate and maintain, it responds well to fertilizing and pruning. It is a quick grower and it is advisable to use a pot slightly bigger than necessary and repot regularly each spring. A lover of light, it can be kept in full sun, except for the hottest part of summer. Protect in winter.

21 CERCIS SILIQUASTRUM L.

A small tree with a range originally in the western part of Asia Minor, the Judas tree is now found wild in Mediterranean countries.

Repotting Every 2–3 years in autumn or early spring, with a mixture of 70% soil and 30% coarse sand or equivalent material.

Pruning and wiring The first drastic pruning should be carried out to coincide with repotting and selective trimming of the foliage. Reduce the new shoots to 1–2 leaves before flowering and during the entire growing period. Wire in late spring to early autumn. The branches are flexible but rather fragile; proceed gradually and carefully.

Feeding Early spring to autumn once every 20–30 days.

Notes The Judas tree enjoys light and full sun, but should be protected during winter in very cold areas. Because the pruning cuts are not easily covered by scar tissue, it is best to protect them with a sealing compound. Eliminate any suckers sprouting from the base of the trunk as soon as they appear. Likewise pick off the fruits. Water only when the soil is completely dried out. Leaves may be removed from healthy, well-fed plants from early to mid June.

22 CHAENOMELES SPECIOSA Nakai

This shrub and its many cultivars, originally from China, is widely cultivated for ornamental purposes.

Repotting Every 3–4 years in autumn or early spring, with 70% soil and 30% coarse sand or equivalent material.

Pruning and wiring The first pruning of the roots should coincide with repotting and reduction of aerial part, preferably in autumn. Cut back the new shoots, shortening them to the first 2 leaves, in late spring after flowering.

Feeding Once every two weeks from early spring to flowering, then every 30 days with a gap during the hottest part of summer.

Notes Valued for its precocious and abundant spring flowers, it is suitable for cultivation mainly in the *kabudachi* (clump) style. Once the clump is established, eliminate immediately any suckers sprouting from the trunk base. Protect during winter, if possible in the greenhouse.

23 CHAMAECYPARIS OBTUSA Endl.

Originally from Japan, where it grows in nature to as much as 120 ft (35 m), it is held to be sacred by devotees of Shinto. It has numerous cultivars and dwarf varieties and is widely used for ornamental purposes outside its native areas as well. This tree is quite long-lived.

Repotting In spring every 3–4 years, with 80% humus-rich, lime-free soil and 20% coarse sand or equivalent material.

Pruning and wiring Carry out the first pruning of the roots at the same time as repotting in spring, or even better while selectively trimming the foliage. Shape and thicken the aerial part by pinching out the still-tender new shoots with the fingers. Wiring of trunk and branches can be done at any time of year, preferably at least 3 months after repotting.

Feeding Every 20 days during spring, late summer and early autumn

Notes This lime-hating plant needs cool, fertile soil. Avoid lime-rich water by using rain or distilled water. Avoid exposure to direct sunlight in summer and spray the foliage once or twice a day. The soil must never be permitted to dry out completely.

---

24 CORYLUS AVELLANA L. var. 'CONTORTA'

A cultivar widely distributed for ornament, with unusually twisted branches, this hazel may grow to 10 ft (3 m). It is particularly attractive in winter when the development of the trunk and branches is clearly visible because of the absence of leaves and the presence of pendulous male catkins.

Repotting Every 2–3 years in autumn or spring, with 70% soil and 30% coarse sand or equivalent material.

Pruning and wiring The first pruning of the root system should be done preferably in autumn at the same time as repotting and pruning of the top. Reduce new shoots to 1–2 leaves during the growing season. Position trunk and branches with wire in spring and summer.

Feeding Every 20–30 days from early spring to autumn, with a gap of about 40 days during midsummer.

Notes A very resistant and adaptable plant, it usually creates no special problems, although its suitability as a bonsai is debatable. Avoid prolonged and direct exposure to sunlight in summer; eliminate, as soon as they show, any suckers at the base of the trunk and branches. Never allow the soil to dry out entirely.

25 CRATAEGUS CUNEATA Sieb. et Zucc.

A shrub originally from China and Japan, particularly prized for its wealth of white flowers followed by a profusion of small red fruits. Cultivars with red flowers have recently been used as bonsai in Japan.

Repotting Every 2–3 years in early spring or autumn, with 70% soil and 30% coarse sand or equivalent material.

Pruning and wiring The first major treatment of the root system should be carried out at the time of repotting and selective reduction of the crown – preferably in early spring. Always leave a strong root system; if this is not possible with a single pruning, reduce it gradually with each repotting. In spring trim the new shoots back to the first 2 leaves. Position the trunk and branches during growth, from spring to summer.

Feeding Once every 20–30 days from early spring to autumn, stopping for a month during midsummer.

Notes A comparatively easy plant to cultivate, there may be some rooting problems if the periods mentioned above are not observed. Protect from direct and prolonged exposure to sunlight in summer and avoid the soil drying out completely.

---

26 CRYPTOMERIA JAPONICA D. Don

An evergreen conifer originally from China and Japan, the Japanese cedar may form entire forests. It has awl-like leaves in spirals which can take on reddish tints in winter.

Repotting Every 3–5 years in spring after growth has begun, with 70% soil and 30% coarse sand or equivalent material.

Pruning and wiring Pruning of the roots should be carried out gradually a year after selective trimming of the foliage. To shape and thicken the aerial part, pinch new shoots with the fingers during the growth season. Position trunk and branches immediately after reduction of the foliage, in spring and summer. Protect the plant from sun and wind after pruning and wiring. Spray with water several times daily.

Feeding Every 20–30 days from spring to autumn.

Notes The plant is sensitive to winter frosts and must be protected under glass. In summer never let the soil dry out completely and spray the foliage. Because the Japanese cedar has a tendency to develop a thickened trunk at the junction with the branches, it is helpful to remove unwanted upper branches as soon as possible.

27   CUPRESSUS SEMPERVIRENS L.

Cultivated since antiquity, the Italian cypress is a very long-lived tree, growing throughout the Mediterranean basin. It comes in two forms: f. *sempervirens* (columnar in habit) and f. *horizontalis*, with distinctly layered branches.

Repotting Every 2–3 years in spring or end summer, with 60% earth and 40% coarse sand or equivalent material.

Pruning and wiring It is advisable to carry out initial pruning of the roots to coincide with repotting and reduction of foliage in summer (end of summer early autumn). Thicken the foliage mass either by pinching out the still-tender young shoots or trimming with scissors during growth. When repotting the following year, from autumn to spring, carry out wiring for positioning trunk and branches.

Feeding Once a month from spring to autumn.

Notes This is a strongly growing tree and it is best to repot young specimens every other year, and older ones every third year. Avoid letting the soil dry out completely and protect during winter. Whereas the *sempervirens* form is suitable for creating clumps, f. *horizontalis* is better as an individual specimen.

---

28   CYCAS REVOLUTA Thunb.

Originally from southern Japan, this is one of the smallest representatives of the genus.

Repotting Every 3–4 years in late spring, with 60% soil and 40% coarse sand or equivalent material.

Pruning and wiring The fairly superficial root system does not generally require severe pruning. If it is done, the work must be carried out in summer and the plant firmly fixed at least until the following spring. During subsequent repottings, simply shorten the smaller roots slightly. To improve the look of the plant, resort to wires or to ties that bend the leaf tip downwards. The same result can be obtained by pressing the soft leaf repeatedly with the fingers.

Feeding From spring to autumn once every 30 days. The plant also benefits from iron-based products applied three or four times in spring–summer.

Notes It does well indoors in a bright position, but avoid exposure to direct sun and spray the foliage once or twice a day. Water only when the soil is partially dry. Get rid of dry leaves by cutting off the stalks. If kept outdoors in mild areas, protect during the winter, preferably in the greenhouse.

29 **CYDONIA OBLONGA** Miller

The quince is a tree originating in northern Iran and trans-Caucasian regions. It has deciduous, ovate, short-stalked leaves, fluffy gray-green beneath, the upper side dark green. The flowers are pinkish white, single, with 5 petals. The round golden-yellow fruits are strongly scented.

Repotting Every 2–3 years in spring, with 70% soil and 30% coarse sand.

Pruning and wiring Drastic pruning of the root system for positioning needs to be done at the same time as repotting and reduction of the foliage, eliminating those branches not needed for the final design of the plant. Shorten the new shoots in summer or late autumn. Position the trunk and branches in spring, but at least 3 months after repotting.

Feeding Once a month in spring and autumn. In the latter season use mainly products higher in phosphorus and potassium.

Notes Keep in full sun, but do not let the soil dry out completely. Spray the foliage periodically. Protect under glass in winter.

30 **DIANTHUS CARTHUSIANORUM** L.

A herbaceous perennial which in nature takes the form of a hemispherical cushion of branches covered by straight leaves, pointed at the tip. A thick tap-root joins the aerial part to the rest of the root system. The fairly small flowers are pink, solitary, and 5-petalled.

Repotting Shorten the new shoots during the growing season, taking care to eliminate dry leaves around the branches. Wiring is not usually necessary. Fix the plant firmly in the pot during transplanting to encourage rooting.

Feeding Every 25–30 days from early spring to autumn, halting for about 40 days during midsummer.

Notes There are two possible uses of this species:

– as an accompaniment to other plants, in which case the aerial part should have direct contact with the soil when planting.

– as a bonsai. Leave the tap-root uncovered as this stimulates the trunk, and arrange the root system in a bonsai container. The result is a plant which is a little outside the classic scheme but which is easy to cultivate and attractive to look at.

31 DIOSPYROS KAKI L. f.

Chinese persimmons are small trees, sometimes shrubs, originally from the Far East – China, Japan, and Korea. They are appreciated and grown in many lands for their edible fruit.
Repotting Every 2–3 years, with a mixture of 70% soil and 30% coarse sand or equivalent material.
Pruning and wiring The first proper pruning of the roots should be carried out at the same time as repotting and reduction of the aerial part. Shape the crown in the growing season, reducing the new and still-tender shoots to 2 leaves. Wire to position the trunk and branches from spring to summer, protecting the bark because the wood will still be rather fragile.
Feeding Once every 20–30 days from early spring to autumn, halting for about one month in midsummer.
Notes Because the wounds – especially the bigger ones – do not form scar tissue easily, they must be sealed with a special compound. Use, where possible, young plants, and shape by pruning new shoots and wiring. Never allow the soil to dry out completely and keep in a sunny position. Protect in winter.

---

32 EHRETIA MICROPHYLLA Lam.

An evergreen shrub from tropical Asia with dark green oval leaves, shiny above, paler beneath. The small flowers are white, followed by berries that are red when ripe.
Repotting Outside its native range, once every 2–3 years in late spring, with 60% humus-rich soil, 10% peat, and 30% coarse sand or equivalent material.
Pruning and wiring Carry out pruning of the roots to coincide with repotting and subsequent reduction of the aerial part. Shorten the shoots to the first 2 leaves during growth. Wire at the same time, or in late summer. Make sure the wire does not remain on the plant for more than 3 months.
Feeding Every 15–20 days from early spring to autumn, with a pause of about 40 days during midsummer. Apply fertilizer as well in winter once a month.
Notes The plant is particularly sensitive to sudden changes of temperature, so it needs to be kept in a bright and sheltered spot. It can be taken outdoors in late spring and summer. Avoid exposure to direct sun and temperatures below 60°F (15°C). The soil should never be allowed to dry out completely. Indoors spray the foliage daily.

33 ELAEAGNUS MULTIFLORA Thunb.

Originally from the Far East – China, Japan, and Korea – the oleaster is a medium-sized shrub with deciduous leaves, green above and silvery below. The small scented flowers are followed by oblong drupes which are red when ripe, persisting throughout the winter.

Repotting Every 2–3 years in early spring, with 70% soil, 10% peat, and 20% coarse sand or equivalent material.

Pruning and wiring Initial pruning of the roots should coincide with repotting and reduction of the foliage after flowering. Always leave a good root system, repeating the operation every successive year until the required proportions are achieved. Shorten the new shoots at the start of or during the summer, reducing them to the first 2 leaves. Position the trunk and branches in summer at least 3 months after repotting.

Feeding Once every 20–30 days from early spring to autumn, halting for around a month during midsummer.

Notes This is a highly disease-resistant and easily cultivated plant. Because the wounds do not easily form scar tissue, it is advisable, where possible, to shape the crown by pruning the shoots. Never allow the soil to dry out entirely and protect during the winter.

---

34 EUONYMUS ALATUS Sieb.

Originating in the Far East – China and Japan – this is a medium-sized shrub distinguishable by the marked suberose "wings" which grow on the branches when the plant matures. It is cultivated for ornamental purposes, both for this feature and for the fiery red autumn leaves.

Repotting Every 2–3 years during spring or autumn, with 70% soil and 30% coarse sand or equivalent material.

Pruning and wiring Carry out:
– first pruning of the roots at the same time as repotting and selective reduction of the crown;
– pruning to shape in late spring to early summer after flowering, reducing the new shoots to 2 leaves;
– wiring from spring to summer, protecting the bark from the wire.

Feeding Every 20–30 days from early spring to autumn, with one month's rest during midsummer.

Notes The soil should not be left to dry out completely. In summer avoid prolonged exposure to sunlight. When the time comes for fruiting it is essential to have several specimens near one another so as to achieve cross-pollination as flowers can be bisexual or unisexual. Protect in winter.

35 EUPHORBIA BALSAMIFERA Ait.

This succulent plant with a typical candelabra shape comes from East Africa, the Canary Islands, and southern Arabia.
Repotting Every 2 years in late spring, with 50% soil and 50% coarse sand.
Pruning and wiring It is necessary to treat the roots and branches with great care. The roots should be slightly shortened in the course of repotting, the branches from late spring to early autumn, but limited to the absolute minimum. Wiring is not as a rule necessary, but can be effected with great care in late spring.
Feeding Every 20–30 days during the growth period from spring to autumn.
Notes Unusual and perhaps debatable as a bonsai, it can do well as a house plant without creating too many problems. Water only when the soil is dry. The plant will benefit from not being exposed for too long to direct sunlight during the summer. Do not water for at least two weeks after repotting and when the plant is dropping leaves.
 The cut branches emit a latex which should be removed with warm water before it solidifies.

36 FAGUS CRENATA Bl.

The tree is originally from Japan and resembles the European beech, *F. sylvatica*, but has ash-gray bark and narrower leaves.
Repotting Every 2–3 years in early spring, with 70% soil, 10% peat, and 20% coarse sand or equivalent material.
Pruning and wiring Initial pruning of the root system will be done to coincide with repotting. Reduce the roots gradually repeating the procedure every 2 years until the desired height is attained. Prune the foliage to shape in late spring, leaving 2–3 leaves. Position the trunk and branches from spring to autumn, taking care to protect the bark.
Feeding Every 20–30 days from early spring to autumn, with a halt of around a month during midsummer.
Notes The soil should not be allowed to dry out completely. Because it is a plant with strong tip development, branches should be proportionately pruned more drastically towards the apex, in order to stimulate vegetation lower down. Leaves may be removed from early to mid June, but only on healthy, well-fed plants.

37   FAGUS SYLVATICA L.

The European beech is a medium-sized tree which grows principally in mountain regions from Europe to the Caucasus. It has smooth gray bark and ovate-elliptical deciduous leaves with wavy margins, short-stalked and briefly pointed at the tip.

Repotting In autumn or spring; younger specimens every 2–3 years, older ones every 3–4 years, with 70% soil, 10% peat, and 20% coarse sand or equivalent materials.

Pruning and wiring Carry out initial pruning for positioning the roots at the same time as repotting and reduction of aerial part, preferably in autumn. If these operations are done in spring, restrict them to shortening of the bigger roots. Shape the crown either by pinching out the still tender new shoots at the beginning of the growing period or by reducing to 2–3 leaves in late spring. Wire from spring to late summer, taking care to protect the bark.

Feeding Every 25–30 days from early spring to autumn, with a rest in midsummer.

Notes Expose in a bright place, but avoid direct sunlight from late spring to end of summer. Do not let the soil dry out entirely. In pruning the crown, bear in mind the apical predominance.

38   FICUS BENJAMINA L.

Originating over a vast area ranging from India to northern Australia, the weeping fig is widely cultivated here and elsewhere as a house plant. It has smooth gray bark, branches that tend to droop, and ovate, entire, glossy leaves with a pointed tip.

Repotting Outside its native range, every 2–3 years in late spring, with 60% soil, 10% peat, and 30% coarse sand.

Pruning and wiring The first proper pruning should be carried out at the same time as repotting and reduction of the foliage. If there is no sign of satisfactory rooting, remove the leaves entirely. Reduce the new shoots to 2 leaves in late spring–early summer. Wiring can be effected at any time of year, but protect the bark. Since *F. benjamina* is quite vigorous, watch regularly to make sure wires do not cut into growing branches.

Feeding Every 20–30 days from early spring to autumn, and a couple of times during autumn–winter.

Notes It is one of the most adaptable of house plants which can even stand poor conditions of light. Avoid sudden changes of temperature and light, and, if possible, expose during spring and summer – though not for too long – to sunlight. In autumn–winter water only when the soil becomes partially dry.

39 FICUS CARICA L.

The common fig is a small tree, sometimes a shrub, with smooth grayish bark, deciduous, alternate, petiolate, rough, and normally palmate leaves, dark green above and paler green below. Renowned and cultivated for its fruit, its was originally from Asia Minor but is found growing wild in the Mediterranean region.

Repotting Every 2–3 years in early spring, with 70% soil and 30% coarse sand.

Pruning and wiring Initial pruning of the roots should be carried out in spring to coincide with repotting and selective reduction of the crown. Shorten the new shoots to the first 2 leaves during the growth period, preferably in late spring. At the same time wiring can be done, proceeding with care and protecting the bark.

Feeding Once a month from spring to autumn.

Notes Generally the plant tends to develop progressively smaller leaves when grown in a container, so it is best to remove the biggest leaves. Defoliation is possible with healthy and well-fed plants from early to mid June. Water only when the soil is partially dried out.

---

40 FICUS NERIIFOLIA Sm.

This small tree is easily distinguished by its narrow, lanceolate leaves – somewhat resembling those of a weeping willow – which are bright green.

Repotting Every 2–3 years in early or late spring, with 60% soil, 10% peat, and 30% coarse sand or equivalent material.

Pruning and wiring Carry out the first pruning of the root system at the same time as repotting and reduction of the aerial part. During the growing season shorten the new shoots to the first 2 leaves. Wiring can be effected at any time of year, protecting the bark.

Feeding From spring to autumn every 25–30 days; in autumn and winter every 40–60 days.

Notes The plant is particularly lovely and suitable for growing as a bonsai or mame bonsai, developing an interesting trunk base and aerial roots within a few years. Avoid sudden changes of temperature and spray the foliage at least once a day during the summer with water at room temperature. Allow the soil to dry out partially between waterings, especially in winter. If kept outside, protect the plant from temperatures below 60°F (15°C).

41   FICUS RELIGIOSA L.

The bo tree, originally from India, is regarded as sacred by Hindus and Buddhists. It has narrow, heart-shaped leaves, with a long tip; new leaves are pink.

Repotting Every 2–3 years in spring, before the buds begin to swell, with 60% soil, 10% peat, and 30% coarse sand.

Pruning and wiring Carry out initial pruning of the root system at the same time as selective trimming of the aerial part and repotting. Reduce the new shoots to 2 leaves during the growing season. The trunk and branches may be positioned at any time of year, but preferably from autumn to spring. Protect the bark when wiring and check frequently to make sure the wire is not cutting into rapidly growing branches.

Feeding Once a month from spring to autumn and every other month from autumn to spring.

Notes This is a plant for the greenhouse or indoors, which has to live in a very bright position and be protected from temperature fluctuations. Spray the foliage at least once a day from spring to summer and from time to time during the rest of the year. In summer, when the temperature climbs to around 69°–77°F (20°–25°C), it should be exposed gradually to direct sunlight.

---

42   FICUS RETUSA L.

The plant's original range extends from southern China to the Philippines, Borneo, and Malaysia. It is of compact growth, with coriaceous, glossy, obovate leaves to 4 in (10 cm). It is very popular as a bonsai in its native lands.

Repotting Every 2–3 years in late spring – when temperatures are around 68°F (20°C) – with a mixture of 60% soil, 10% peat, and 30% coarse sand.

Feeding Reduction of the aerial part should coincide with the first repotting and pruning of the root system. In regions with a temperate climate these operations need to be effected gradually, protecting the plant for at least a month after repotting. Thicken and shape the foliage by reducing the new shoots to 2 leaves during late spring–summer. Wiring may be done at any season, but at least 3 months after repotting. Protect the bark.

Feeding Every 20–30 days from spring to autumn and every 40–60 days at other times of the year.

Notes The plant is highly sensitive to sudden changes of temperature which may cause all the leaves to drop. In winter keep it in a bright, warm place or in the greenhouse. Indoors, spray the foliage at least once daily with water at room temperature. Water when the soil becomes partly dry.

43 FRAXINUS CHINENSIS Roxb.

A dioecious tree of medium height originally from China, Korea, and Japan, it has deciduous, imparipinnate leaves. It is prized for its autumn color, the leaves turning violet red, and for its scented pendulous inflorescences in spring.

Repotting Every 2–3 years in spring, with 60% soil, 20% peat, and 20% coarse sand or equivalent material.

Pruning and wiring Carry out the first severe pruning of the roots at the same time as repotting and selective trimming of the crown. Shorten the new shoots to the first 2 leaves during the summer. Wire the trunk and branches from spring to summer, protecting the bark.

Feeding Every 20–30 days from spring to autumn, with an interval during midsummer.

Notes The soil should not be left to dry out completely. If kept indoors, the foliage must be sprayed in spring and summer at least once a day. The plant will benefit from direct exposure, though not for too long, to sunlight from late spring to autumn. For aesthetic reasons, the leaves may be reduced to the first four leaflets.

44 FRAXINUS ORNUS L.

The manna ash is a small tree, or more frequently a shrub, originally from southern Europe and Asia Minor. The bark is pale gray, the leaves deciduous, opposite, and imparipinnate. The white scented flowers are in terminal panicles.

Repotting Every 2–3 years in autumn or early spring, with a mixture of 60% soil, 20% peat, and 20% coarse sand.

Pruning and wiring Prune the root system and aerial part during the first repotting. Thicken and shape the crown by shortening the new shoots in the growing season and by pruning the branches back to just above the buds during the winter rest period. Position the trunk and branches from spring to late summer.

Feeding From early spring to autumn once every 20–30 days, with an interval during midsummer.

Notes This is a highly resilient plant which roots easily even when these are drastically pruned. Expose to full sun so as to obtain smaller leaves and shorter internodes, but keep watch on the soil to ensure it does not get completely dry.

45 GINKGO BILOBA L.

Introduction – see p. 93.

Repotting Major work on the root system should be carried out in early spring, when the buds are swelling and before the plant starts to grow. Because it produces a large number of roots, the ginkgo should be repotted at least every 2 years. The soil, which should include 40% coarse sand or similar material, must be well drained.

Pruning and wiring Avoid severe pruning of old branches which never completely form scar tissue. It is advisable, therefore, to follow these procedures in shaping the plant:
– prune the new shoots, leaving only 2 leaves, during the growing season, preferably in spring;
– prune the new branches, leaving 2–3 buds.

Wiring should be done from spring to autumn and it is essential periodically to check that it does not cut into the bark.

Feeding Repeat at two-week intervals from early spring to the beginning of summer and from early September to end October.

Notes A plant of temperate climes, the ginkgo, particularly its roots, must be protected from prolonged frost. Because removal of the leaves does not give appreciable results, the only way to reduce the foliage is to expose the plant to sun in spring and, at the same time, water sparingly.

---

46 HOLARRHENA ANTIDYSENTERICA Wall.

An evergreen tree or, more frequently, shrub from India, Pakistan, and West Africa. The bark is brown, scaly, and exudes a milky latex. The leaves are ovate with a pointed tip and the white flowers are borne in a terminal corymb.

Repotting Every 2–3 years in spring (end March–April), with 60% soil, 20% peat, and 20% coarse sand.

Pruning and wiring Outside its range, shorten the roots slightly at each repotting; repeat the operation in following years. Reduce the new shoots to the first 2 leaves from late spring to end summer. At the same time carry out the wiring, protecting the bark.

Feeding Every 20–30 days from spring to autumn and a couple of times during autumn–winter.

Notes A hothouse or indoor plant, it benefits from direct exposure to sunlight during late spring and summer with a temperature around 77°F (25°C). Water plentifully and spray the foliage frequently throughout the year, especially in summer.

47　JACARANDA MIMOSIFOLIA D. Don.

This tree, originally from tropical America, fairly long-lived, has opposite, bipinnate leaves, up to 18 in (45 cm) long. It is cultivated for ornament well outside its native range.

Repotting Every 1–2 years in spring, with 60% soil, 10% peat, and 30% coarse sand or equivalent material.

Pruning and wiring Initial pruning of the root system can be done at the same time as repotting and reduction of the aerial part. Shorten the new shoots, leaving at least the first pair of leaves on the branch or pinching them out when they are still tender. Wiring may be carried out at any season, but outside its original range the best time is from spring to summer.

Feeding Once every 20–25 days from spring to autumn.

Notes It is fairly frequently used as a bonsai in countries with a tropical climate, particularly in the *kabudachi* (clump) style. Never allow the soil to dry out completely and avoid direct and prolonged exposure to sunlight in midsummer. If kept indoors, spray the foliage at least once daily. It enjoys a bright position.

48　JASMINUM NUDIFLORUM Lindl.

This shrub, originally from western China, is widely grown outside its native range for its beautiful flowers.

Repotting Every 1–2 years, preferably in autumn after the leaves fall or in early spring, with 70% soil, 20% coarse sand, and 10% peat.

Pruning and wiring The root system should be pruned preferably in autumn in the course of initial repotting and selective reduction of the aerial part. Prune the branches after flowering; afterwards shorten the new shoots; repeat the operation in late summer. Always leave at least a few leaflets or buds on the branch. Carry out wiring after flowering; protect the bark and proceed carefully to avoid breaking the rather fragile branches.

Feeding Once every 20 days from early spring to flowering, then once a month until autumn, with a halt of about 50 days in midsummer.

Notes The plant likes full sun and moist soil, but avoid direct and prolonged exposure to the sun during summer. At the same time spray the foliage occasionally. Eliminate any suckers that may appear at the base of the trunk. Protect during winter.

49   **JUNIPERUS RIGIDA** Sieb. et Zucc.

A small tree or shrub originally from China, Korea, and Japan. The Japanese know and use various cultivars as bonsai. In morphology it is very similar to *Juniperus communis*, but differs from it in a few details, such as the stiffness of the needles (hence the specific name), the drooping habit of the thinner branches, and the winter color.

Repotting Every 2–3 years in late spring, when the plant is already growing, with 70% soil and 30% coarse sand. If the pot is relatively shallow, reduce the earth by 10% and add the same proportion of peat.

Pruning and wiring In the course of the first repotting get rid of all branches which are not indispensable to the final design. Shorten the tap-root and thicker roots gradually. To shape and thicken the crown, pinch out the still-tender new shoots with the nails, reducing the apical portion by about two thirds. Wiring is possible at any time of the year, except in spring.

Feeding Once every 20 days from early spring to early summer, and every 30 days from summer to autumn.

Notes The plant lends itself to spectacular *jin* and *shari* treatments. It needs full sunlight and slightly moist soil. It is also essential to spray the foliage from spring to the end of summer.

---

50   **JUNIPERUS SARGENTII** Tak.

Originally from Japan, the Kurile Islands, and the Sahalin peninsula, this juniper appears in nature as a prostrate, groundcover plant which generally grows among rocks and near the sea. It has squamous dark green leaves and bluish berries.

Repotting Every 3–4 years from spring to autumn, with 60% soil, 10% peat, and 30% coarse sand or equivalent material.

Pruning and wiring Carry out root reduction gradually in the course of repotting, at least every other year. Shape the crown exclusively by pinching out the still-tender young shoots in the growing season. Get rid of undesirable branches, both while repotting and during growth. Wiring may be done at any season, but preferably from autumn to winter.

Feeding From early spring to autumn every 20–30 days, stopping for about a month and a half in midsummer.

Notes Protect the plant for at least 2 months after repotting. Keep it in a very bright place but avoid direct and prolonged exposure to sun between late spring and summer. During this time spray the foliage frequently. Do not let the soil dry out completely and shelter under glass in winter.

51 LAGERSTROEMIA INDICA L.

The crape myrtle is a small tree or large shrub with deciduous leaves, originally from China and Korea, widely utilized for ornamental purposes. A particularly interesting feature is the smooth, light brown trunk, mottled when mature.

Repotting Every 1–2 years from early spring to summer, with plenty of humus, and 30% coarse sand or equivalent material.

Pruning and wiring Drastic work on the roots should be undertaken at the time of repotting, always leaving a strong root structure; the operation may be repeated in following years until the desired height is attained. Pruning should be carried out at the beginning of the dormant period, in autumn, so as to stimulate flower production the next year. Shorten the shoots only after flowering. Position the trunk and branches with wire from spring to autumn, protecting the bark and proceeding with care.

Feeding Every 20–30 days from spring to autumn.

Notes The plant needs frequent watering in spring, but at other times only when the soil becomes partially dry. It does reasonably well indoors provided it is given a bright position. Outside it can be exposed directly to the sun. Protect under glass in winter.

52 LARIX DECIDUA Miller

The European larch grows from the Alps to the Carpathians, where it often forms pure woods. A colonizing species, the tree may be found above the altitude of 8,200 ft (2,500 m). It bears yellow male flowers and erect, red female flowers.

Repotting Every 3–4 years in spring, before the needles emerge, or in late summer, with a mixture of 60% soil, 10% peat, and 30% coarse sand.

Pruning and wiring Eliminate the unwanted branches, to encourage rooting, in the course of initial repotting and at the same time reduce the root system, which should remain fairly compact. Shorten the shoots during the growth season. The branches can also be reduced in autumn–winter, always leaving at least 2–3 buds. Carry out wiring from late spring to autumn.

Feeding Every 25–30 days from spring to autumn, with an interval of about a month and a half during midsummer.

Notes Very hardy even in climatic conditions different from that of its origins; but when raised in a container it should be protected from direct and prolonged exposure to sunlight in summer. During this season spray the foliage occasionally in the evening. Eliminate any suckers from the base of the branches.

53   **LARIX KAEMPFERI** Carr.

The Japanese larch differs from the European larch by having larger, sea-green needles, ovoid cones, and reddish shoots. Originally from Japan, it is widely cultivated elsewhere.

Repotting Every 2–3 years for young specimens, 3–4 years for older ones, in early spring. Use a mixture of 60% soil, 20% peat, and 20% coarse sand or equivalent material.

Pruning and wiring The first drastic pruning of the roots should be carried out at the time of repotting or reduction of the aerial part. Proceed gradually, always leaving a sufficient root mass. Prune the shoots during growth to shape and thicken the crown. Do the wiring from summer to autumn.

Feeding Once every 25–30 days from early spring to autumn, stopping during the heat of midsummer.

Notes The trunk and branches are easily positioned by wiring, but be careful not to damage the buds. Keep in a bright place but avoid direct and prolonged exposure to sun during the summer. Although water must not be allowed to stand in the pot, the soil should be constantly moist.

---

54   **LIGUSTRUM LUCIDUM** Ait.

The glossy privet comes originally from China and was introduced in the eighteenth century to Europe, where it is widely grown. The glossy leaves are pointed, dark green above and paler green below.

Repotting Every 2–3 years in early spring, with 60% soil, 10% peat, and 30% coarse sand or equivalent material.

Pruning and wiring The first proper pruning of the roots will coincide with repotting and selective trimming of the crown. Reduce new shoots throughout the year to the first 2 leaves, thus encouraging denser foliage growth. Position the trunk and branches with wire from spring to autumn, protecting the bark.

Feeding Once every 20 days in early spring and autumn; every 30 days in late spring and summer.

Notes A sun-loving plant, easy to shape and maintain. It adapts well to indoor life provided it is given a bright position. The soil must never be allowed to become absolutely dry. Bear in mind that the plant has a tendency to lose its pruned branches when it is not growing.

55 LIGUSTRUM SINENSE Lour.

Originally from China, this privet bears more flowers than others, followed by showy berries.

Repotting Every 2–3 years in early spring, with a mixture of 60% soil, 10% peat, and 30% coarse sand or equivalent material.

Pruning and wiring The plant can withstand fairly drastic pruning of the roots at the same time as repotting and reduction of the aerial part. Shape the foliage in late spring or early autumn after flowering, shortening the shoots to the first 2 leaves. Wiring is possible at any season but is particularly advisable in late summer.

Feeding Every 20 days from early spring to flowering and afterwards every 30 days until late autumn, with an interval in midsummer.

Notes This plant is especially attractive in flower, stands up well to pruning and creates no particular problems. Keep in full sun but avoid, when in a container, prolonged and direct exposure to sunlight in summer. Protect under glass in winter.

56 LIQUIDAMBAR FORMOSANA Hance

This tree originated in central China. It has leaves with 3–5 lobes, rough underneath, and reddish in spring and autumn.

Repotting Every 2–3 years in early spring or autumn, with 60% soil, 20% peat, and 20% coarse sand.

Pruning and wiring During the initial repotting, prune both the root system and the crown. Successive prunings of branches should be carried out in spring or autumn. Reduce the still-tender new shoots to the first 2 leaves. Wire the trunk and branches from spring to autumn, protecting the bark.

Feeding Once every 20–30 days from early spring to autumn, stopping in midsummer.

Notes Although this is a sun-loving plant, it has to be protected from direct and long exposure in summer. Never allow the soil to dry out completely and spray the foliage often in summer. Protect under glass in winter. With healthy, well-fed plants, it is possible to remove leaves from early to mid June.

57 **MABA BUXIFOLIA** (Rottb.) Pers.

An evergreen plant originally from tropical Southeast Asia, with small leathery leaves, initially reddish, then deep green. The bark is a lovely dark gray, almost violet, color. It has small white flowers and round black fruits.

Repotting Every 3–4 years in spring, with 70% soil and 30% coarse sand or equivalent material.

Pruning and wiring Carry out major pruning of the roots at the time of repotting and selective trimming of the crown. Outside its native range, pruning of the roots should be gradual and repeated while repotting; eventually it will be restricted to eliminating the roots above the drainage holes and along the rims of the pot. Carry out wiring from spring to summer.

Feeding From spring to early autumn every 30 days and a couple of times in autumn–winter.

Notes An indoor or hothouse plant which can nevertheless stand lower than original temperatures. Expose to direct sunlight whenever the temperature rises above 68°F (20°C) and never allow the soil to dry out completely.

---

58 **MALUS HALLIANA** Koehne

This small tree comes from China but is not found growing wild there; it has long since been introduced to Japan. The flowers are pinkish white, red in bud, and the fruits are long-stemmed pomes, purplish when ripe.

Repotting It is advisable to repot every year in early spring, with 70% soil, 10% peat, and 20% coarse sand or equivalent material.

Pruning and wiring Positional pruning of the roots should coincide with repotting and selective reduction of the crown. Shorten the new shoots after flowering in late spring. Carry out wiring from spring to autumn, but at least 2 months after repotting.

Feeding Every 20–30 days from end of spring to autumn.

Notes This is a sturdy plant, prized in spring for its flowers and in autumn–early winter for the persistent fruits which remain after the leaves drop. For a better aesthetic effect and in order not to wear out the plant, it is best to be selective about fruit distribution, getting rid of some. The soil should be well drained and never completely dry.

59　MALUS PUMILA Miller

The crab apple tree has an enormous range that includes Europe and part of Asia, and is nowadays cultivated and found growing wild in other continents as well. The 5-petalled flowers are pink or white, and the pomes vary in color: green, yellow or red.

Repotting Every 1–2 years in early spring. The plant is not especially demanding as to soil and it is advisable to add 10% peat and 20% coarse sand.

Pruning and wiring Carry out root pruning at the same time as initial repotting and selective trimming of the crown. Reduce the new shoots after flowering. The next year, in late winter, prune the branches, leaving at least 1–2 buds. Position the trunk and branches from spring to summer, protecting the bark.

Feeding Every 15–20 days from early spring to early autumn. Do not fertilize repotted plants for at least 3 months.

Notes Older specimens can be repotted every 2–3 years. Never allow the soil to dry out completely; protect the plant from direct and prolonged exposure to sunlight in summer and from frosts during winter.

60　MILLETTIA JAPONICA A. Gray

This small climbing shrub with evergreen leaves, originally from Japan, is similar to wisteria, but differs in that it has a smaller trunk, and smaller leaves and flowers. The variety *microphylla* (Makino) is also known and used as a bonsai.

Repotting Every 1–2 years in early spring, with 80% soil and 20% coarse sand or equivalent material.

Pruning and wiring Shorten the roots while repotting. Pruning to shape and form the crown should be done in autumn, after leaf fall. Reduce the new shoots after flowering, in summer. Wiring can be carried out from spring to autumn.

Feeding Every 15–20 days from early spring to autumn, using one third of the dose recommended by makers.

Notes Because this plant requires a lot of water, it must be applied regularly, and in winter as well, albeit less frequently. In summer the pot can be placed in a bowl so that the roots can come into contact with the water. Protect in winter.

61 MORUS ALBA L.

Originally from China, where it has been cultivated for thousands of years as food for silkworms, the mulberry is grown well outside its native range. A fairly long-lived tree, its leaves are generally very big.

Repotting As a rule every year, but old specimens can be repotted every other year, with 60% soil and 40% coarse sand or equivalent material.

Pruning and wiring Pruning of the roots should be carried out to coincide with repotting. Pinch out the still-tender shoots in the growing season and prune the branches after flowering. Wire from spring to summer, protecting the bark.

Feeding Every 20–30 days from spring to autumn.

Notes Expose to full sun. Water plentifully during the growing season but make absolutely sure there is no standing water; apply it more sparingly during the brief flowering period. Protect under glass in winter and remove shriveled fruits.

62 MURRAYA PANICULATA Jack

Originally from tropical Asia – Indonesia, India, Philippines, and southern China – the tree has a smooth, light yellow-brown trunk, deep green imparipinnate leaves, racemes of scented, 5-petalled white flowers and long orange-red berries.

Repotting Every 2–3 years in spring, with 50% soil, 20% peat, and 30% coarse sand.

Pruning and wiring In its lands of origin it can withstand drastic root pruning but elsewhere it is best to shorten them by about one third in the course of repotting. Reduce the shoots to the first 2 leaves in late spring or early summer and repeat the operation in late summer. Pruning of the branches and wiring can be undertaken at any time of year.

Feeding Every 20 days from spring to autumn and every 40 days from autumn to spring. Administer an iron-based fertilizer a couple of times during the growing season.

Notes It does well indoors although it is advisable to keep it outside in summer. Spray the foliage frequently and never let the soil dry out completely. The temperature should not drop below 54°F (12°C). Should this happen, the plant may lose all or some of its leaves, which will reform as soon as it is placed in a more suitable spot.

63 MYRTUS COMMUNIS L.

An evergreen tree, or more often a shrub, widely distributed over the Mediterranean region. The leaves are aromatic, ovate with a pointed tip, the axillary white flowers are fragrant and the fruits are blue-black berries.

Repotting Every 2–3 years in spring, with 60% soil and 40% coarse sand or equivalent material.

Pruning and wiring Initial pruning of the roots should take place at the same time as repotting and reduction of the crown. If major work has to be done on the root system, it is best to remove all the leaves to stimulate rooting. Trim the new shoots after flowering, reducing them to the first 2–4 leaves. Position the trunk and branches from spring to autumn, taking care to protect the bark.

Feeding Once every 20–30 days from spring to autumn.

Notes Water abundantly in the spring–summer period, but at other times only when the soil partially dries out. In winter the plant can be brought indoors in a bright but not excessively warm position.

64 OLEA EUROPAEA L.

The olive tree has been cultivated since time immemorial in the Mediterranean area, where some 40 varieties are known, differing from one another in the size of the fruits and leaves. The smooth bark is gray-green when young and later turns gray and becomes fissured.

Repotting Young specimens every 2 years, older ones every 3 years, using 60% soil, 10% peat, and 30% coarse sand or equivalent material.

Pruning and wiring Initial work on the roots should be timed to coincide with repotting and selective reduction of the foliage. If root pruning needs to be drastic, it is advisable to remove the leaves completely to encourage rooting. Reduce the new shoots to the first 2–4 leaves in the growing season. Wire from spring to autumn, protecting the bark.

Feeding Every 20–30 days from spring to autumn. Do not fertilize for 3 months after repotting.

Notes A sun-loving plant which needs to be protected during winter and exposed to full sun in spring and summer, avoiding the soil drying out completely. It can also be kept indoors in a very bright but not excessively warm spot during winter, spraying the foliage daily.

65 OLEA EUROPAEA ssp. OLEASTER DC.

A tree or, more frequently, a shrub, sometimes thorny, of varied behavior but usually with many branches. It is typical of the Mediterranean area, especially scrubland and rocky ground. Regarded as the ancestor of the cultivated olive, it has smaller leaves than the latter and the fruits contain less oil.

Repotting Every 2–3 years in early spring, with a mixture of 60% soil and 40% coarse sand or equivalent material.

Pruning and wiring Cut back the root system gradually or remove all the leaves during repotting, getting rid of any branches unnecessary for the final design. Prune the foliage to shape in the growing season, shortening the new shoots to the first 2–4 leaves. Positional wiring of the trunk and branches can be done the year after repotting from spring to autumn, protecting the bark.

Feeding Every 20–30 days from early spring to autumn.

Notes It makes an ideal bonsai. In regions with mild winters it can be grown in full sun, taking care that the soil never completely dries out. Eliminate any suckers that appear at the base of the trunk or branches. Protect from frosts when in the bonsai container.

---

66 OSTRYA CARPINIFOLIA Scop.

The hop hornbeam is a tree or shrub similar to the hornbeam, with which it often shares the same range. It is a Mediterranean mountain species, growing from southern France to the Caucasus and Asia Minor. It is distinguished by its fruit, enclosed in an involucre, in terminal spikes, similar to that of the hop.

Repotting In spring or autumn, with 60% soil and 40% coarse sand or equivalent material.

Pruning and wiring Pruning to position the roots can be done while repotting and selectively reducing the crown. Branches can also be pruned at the start of the next growing period, always leaving 1–2 buds. Reduce the new shoots, by pinching them out while they are still tender, to the first 2 leaves, and get rid of unwanted buds, removing them before they open. Wiring can be done from spring to summer, protecting the bark.

Feeding In spring and autumn, 3–4 times a year. Increase the frequency of spring feeding if defoliation is under consideration.

Notes Water abundantly during the summer but avoid standing water. Leaves may be removed from healthy and well-fed plants from early to mid June. To obtain lower branches, remove only some of the leaves, concentrating on the higher part of the crown.

67 PHILLYREA ANGUSTIFOLIA L.

An evergreen tree or, more frequently, shrub with Mediterranean distribution. It has opposite, lanceolate leaves, with a pointed tip and entire margins, axillary flowers in greenish-white clusters and round drupes which are black when ripe.

Repotting In early spring, every 2–3 years, with 60% soil and 40% coarse sand or equivalent material.

Pruning and wiring Carry out the initial pruning to position the roots at the same time as repotting, reduction of the crown, and complete leaf removal. For better rooting, protect the plant under glass or cover it with a plastic sheet, spraying periodically. Shorten the new shoots in the growing season. Position the trunk and branches from spring to autumn, taking care to protect the bark.

Feeding Once every 20 days in spring and a couple of times a month in summer–autumn.

Notes Because the plant has some difficulty in rooting, it is advisable to limit root pruning to shortening the roots around the container and above the drainage holes while repotting. Keep the plant in full sun but make sure the soil does not dry out completely. Protect during winter, if possible under glass.

68 PICEA ABIES Karst.

The Norway spruce is widely distributed in Europe from the Alps to Scandinavia and the Balkans. Its reddish bark flakes off in irregular slabs when mature, and the leaves are acicular. There are scores of cultivars.

Repotting Every 3–4 years, with 60% soil, 10% peat, and 30% coarse sand.

Pruning and wiring Carry out initial pruning of the roots while repotting and selectively reducing the crown. Eliminate the smaller branchlets at the base of the branches, as well as those which appear weak and those pointing straight upward or downward, in order to obtain as compact an arrangement of horizontal branches as possible. Shaping and thickening of the foliage can be effected by reducing the still-tender new shoots by two thirds, pinching out with the nails those that are unopened. Carry out wiring from late autumn to winter.

Feeding Every 20–30 days from early spring to summer and from the end of summer to late autumn. Apply an iron-based fertilizer 2–3 times a year.

Notes Await the end of a growth cycle before doing any wiring and, because the small branches are difficult to shape, restrict treatment to the bigger ones. Spray from time to time in the summer and never allow the soil to dry out completely.

69 PICEA GLAUCA 'CONICA'

This small conical white spruce with dense, acicular, pale green foliage, was discovered in 1904 in the Canadian Rocky Mountains near Lake Laggan. It is widely used for ornamental purposes.

Repotting In spring, every 2–3 years for younger specimens, every 3–4 years for older ones, with 60% soil, 10% peat, and 30% coarse sand.

Pruning and wiring Initial pruning to position the root system should coincide with repotting and selective reduction of the crown. To thicken the foliage, eliminate the apical bud from each branch in winter and cut back the still tender new shoots in spring, pinching them out with the nails. Position the trunk and branches in autumn–winter, bending the latter more than necessary because they tend to remain vertical.

Feeding Every 20–30 days in spring and autumn. Administer chelated iron 2–3 times a year.

Notes This tree is particularly adaptable for use as a bonsai because it can stand both repotting and pruning. Select specimens with good features because the plant generally has thin branches and only occasionally a good number growing around the base. Spray the foliage in summer and do not let the soil dry out completely.

---

70 PICEA JEZOENSIS Carr.

This tree is originally from northeast Asia and Japan. It has small pale brown or yellow-brown branches, and flat leaves which are dark green above and light silver green below because of the presence of a pair of stomatal bands.

Repotting In early spring or autumn, every 2–3 years for younger specimens, every 3–5 years for older ones, with 60% soil, 10% peat, and 30% coarse sand or equivalent material.

Pruning and wiring Position the roots, leaving at least two thirds of the root system, and at the same time get rid of any branches not necessary to the final design. Shorten the new shoots by one third or two thirds, proceeding upward or downward, endeavoring to create horizontal layers. Carry out wiring from autumn to winter, at least 3 months after repotting.

Feeding From early spring to summer and from the end of the summer to late autumn. Administer chelated iron once or twice a year.

Notes Tidy the crown once or twice annually, getting rid of dry branches and new shoots at the base of the branches. Spray the foliage during the summer and never allow the soil to dry out completely. In cold climates protect from likely spring frosts.

71　PINUS CEMBRA L.

The arolla pine is a typical mountain pioneering species, originally from the Alps and Carpathians where it grows at altitudes of up to 8,000 ft (2,400 m). It has an erect, pyramidal habit and is very slow-growing and long-lived. The bark is gray, flaking off when mature. The needles, in groups of 5, are flexible, 2–3 in (5–8 cm) long, blue-green with two, thin light bands.

Repotting　Every 4–5 years, in spring or the end of summer, with 60% soil, 10% peat, and 30% coarse sand or equivalent material.

Pruning and wiring　Pruning of the root system should be done carefully after at least a year of acclimatization: merely shorten the bigger roots and always leave a compact root system. Reduce the length of the shoots with the fingers by two thirds, when the needles are clearly distinguishable but before they turn hard. Wire to position the trunk and branches from autumn to winter.

Feeding　Once a month in spring and autumn.

Notes　If the plant is healthy it is possible to get rid of all the shoots before they grow too long. This will stimulate the tree to produce new and denser bundles with shorter needles. Water only when the soil is partially dry. Spray the foliage during the summer.

72　PINUS DENSIFLORA Sieb. et Zucc.

A medium-sized tree originally from Japan, with reddish-brown bark, for which reason it is known as the Japanese red pine. The needles are in pairs, flexible, light green, and 2–5 in (5–12 cm) long.

Repotting　In spring, before the buds open, or in autumn, every 2–3 years for young specimens, every 3–5 years for older ones, with 50% soil, 10% peat, and 40% coarse sand or equivalent material.

Pruning and wiring　Position the roots and eliminate, during initial repotting, any branches not necessary for the final design. Always leave a good root system and repeat the operation in successive years. Thicken the crown by getting rid of two thirds of the new shoots when the needles are well developed but not yet hard. Carry out the wiring from spring to early autumn.

Feeding　Once a month from early to late spring and in autumn. Administer an iron-based fertilizer at least a couple of times a year.

Notes　Water only when the soil is partially dried out. In autumn–winter remove the apical bud of each branch, leaving the lateral buds. If the plant is healthy it is possible to eliminate all the new shoots every 2–3 years before they expand fully. It is necessary, before doing this, to remove some needles from all the branches, leaving a dozen or so near each tip.

73　PINUS MUGO Turra

A small tree, but more often a shrub, from the mountains of central Europe. The stiff needles are in pairs, dark green and 1–1½ in (3–4 cm) long. There are numerous subspecies and varieties which are sometimes hard to classify, because this pine tends to hybridize in the wild. Growth habits of the varieties vary from prostrate kinds with numerous creeping stems, to those with numerous upright stems, or a single, slender trunk. There are also differences in the characteristics of the cones.

Repotting Every 2–3 years for young specimens and every 3–5 years for older ones, in early spring or late summer, using 50% soil and 50% coarse sand.

Pruning and wiring The first positional pruning should be done when repotting and reducing the crown. Always leave a good root system. Reduce the new shoots by two thirds in spring. Carry out wiring at the end of autumn and the beginning of winter.

Feeding Once a month in spring and autumn.

Notes With healthy plants it is possible, in order to increase the number of needles and diminish their size, to get rid of all new shoots every 2 years. Spray the foliage during the summer.

74　PINUS NIGRA Arnold

The Austrian pine comes from the mountains of Austria, Yugoslavia, and Italy. It has a rough, gray-brown or dark brown trunk, and pairs of stiff, pointed, dark green needles, 3–5 in (8–12 cm) long.

Repotting Every 2–3 years for young specimens and every 3–5 years for older ones, in spring or late summer, with 40% soil, 10% peat, and 50% coarse sand or equivalent material.

Pruning and wiring Initial positional pruning of the roots should be done while repotting and selectively reducing the foliage. Proceed gradually, always taking care to leave a strong root system. Subsequent pruning of branches can be done in autumn–winter. Remove from one third to two thirds of shoots in spring, when they are well developed but not yet hard. Position the trunk and branches in autumn–winter.

Feeding Once a month from early to late spring and end of summer to autumn.

Notes To increase needle density, remove the apical bud from each branch, leaving the lateral buds, in late autumn. If the tree is well fed and healthy all the shoots may be eliminated in spring; before doing that, remove the needles from all branches, except for a dozen or so towards the tip.

75 **PINUS PARVIFLORA** Sieb et Zucc.

A tree, or sometimes a large shrub, originally from Japan. The bark of the trunk flakes off in blackish strips and the needles are in bundles of 5, blue-green, curved, flexible and blunt-tipped, 2–3 in (5–7 cm) long. There are more than 150 cultivars – usually reproduced by grafting – which differ mainly in the color and length of the needles. Among so many, special mention should be made of "Himekomatsu Makino," with fairly small blue-green needles, and nowadays certainly the most used.

Repotting In spring or early autumn, every 2–3 years for young specimens and every 3–5 years for older ones, using 50% soil, 10% peat, and 40% coarse sand or equivalent material.

Pruning and wiring Initial pruning to position the roots should be done gradually while repotting. Always leave a good root system. Eliminate any branches unnecessary to the final design when wiring the plant, in autumn–winter. Shorten the new shoots by two thirds during growth, before they harden.

Feeding Once a month from early to late spring and from end of summer to late autumn. Apply chelated iron 2–3 times a year.

Notes Every 1–2 years it is possible to get rid of all the shoots in late spring, on healthy and well-fed trees.

---

76 **PINUS SYLVESTRIS** L.

The Scots pine has a vast range – from Spain to Manchuria, and north as far as the polar circle – with numerous cultivars and geographical races. The scaly bark is reddish brown when young, gray-brown when older. The needles, in pairs, are stiff and often twisted, 1–4 in (3–10 cm) long – generally shorter in southern races – and variable in color from gray-green to blue-green. In Europe it is regarded as the most suitable pine for bonsai.

Repotting Every 3–5 years, in spring or late summer, with 40% soil, 10% peat, and 50% coarse sand.

Pruning and wiring Do the first drastic pruning to position the roots during initial repottings and reduction of aerial part; proceed gradually and always leave a good root system. Shorten the shoots by one third to two thirds in spring. Do wiring in autumn–winter.

Feeding Once a month in spring and autumn.

Notes To obtain more compact growth and to get shorter needles, it is possible, in healthy plants, to get rid of all the shoots in spring, before they harden. Water only when the soil is partially dried out.

77 PINUS THUNBERGII Parl.

Originally from Korea and Japan, this pine has a dark gray or dark pinkish-purple, deeply fissured trunk. The stiff, pointed needles are in pairs, 3–7 in (7–18 cm) long.

Repotting In spring or late summer, every 2–3 years for young specimens and every 3–5 years for older ones, with 40% soil, 10% peat, and 50% coarse sand or equivalent material.

Pruning and wiring The first pruning to position the roots will coincide with repotting and reduction of the crown. Always leave a good root system. Subsequent pruning of the branches can be done when wiring. Shorten the shoots by pinching out when they are still tender, in spring, and eliminate the central buds of each branch in autumn. Wiring can be done at any time except in spring and at least 3 months after repotting.

Feeding Once a month from early spring to autumn. Administer chelated iron at least twice a year.

Notes Spray the crown during the summer. With healthy trees it is possible to eliminate all the shoots every other year, before they harden. Remove all needles that are too long or pendulous and vary exposure of the plant throughout the year so that light can be evenly distributed to the entire foliage.

78 PINUS THUNBERGII Parl. var. 'CORTICOSA' Makino

This is the best-known cultivar of *P. thunbergii*, widely grown in Japan, and usually reproduced by grafting. It has similar leaves to those of the species and is characterized by particularly thick and suberose bark.

Repotting Every 3–5 years, in spring or late summer, with 50% soil and 50% coarse sand or equivalent material.

Pruning and wiring Pruning of the roots should not be too severe, with positioning done in phases while transplanting. It is advisable to leave a strong root system and eventually to use a pot slightly bigger than normal. Remove only one third of the shoots in spring, when they are still soft. Wiring should be carried out from autumn to winter, taking every precaution not to damage the bark.

Feeding Once a month in spring and from the end of summer to late autumn.

Notes The complete removal of the shoots, to reduce the length of the foliage, can be done once every 2–3 years with healthy, strongly-growing trees. Water only when the soil is partly dried out. Spray the crown during the summer.

79 PISTACIA CHINENSIS Bunge

Originally from central and western China, where it grows to a height of 85 ft (25 m), this is usually a large tree with deciduous, pinnate leaves which take on a lovely scarlet color in the autumn. The unisexual flowers are in dense terminal panicles and are followed by small red fruits which turn blue when ripe.

Repotting Every 2–3 years, in spring, with a temperature of about 60°F (15°C), using 50% soil, 20% peat, and 30% coarse sand.

Pruning and wiring Prune the roots while repotting, removing those growing to the edge of the container and above the drainage holes, and if necessary shortening the thicker ones. Prune the branches in late summer and autumn, covering the wounds with a good sealing compound. Reduce the shoots during the growing period. Carry out wiring from spring to summer, protecting the bark and proceeding with caution because the branches are delicate.

Feeding From early spring to late autumn, stopping for about a month during the hottest part of summer.

Notes This is normally considered a house plant, where it should be kept in a bright place with winter temperatures not above 68°F (20°C). Spray the foliage often during growth and water when the soil is partially dried out.

80 PISTACIA LENTISCUS L.

The mastic is an evergreen shrub or, more rarely, a small tree with a range that comprises the Mediterranean lands and the Canary Islands. The bark is brown and scaly, the alternate, paripinnate leaves have blunt-tipped, oval leaflets, the monoecious flowers are in axillary racemes, and the clusters of drupes are red, turning black when ripe.

Repotting Every 2–3 years with young specimens, every 3–4 years with older ones, in spring, with 70% soil and 30% coarse sand.

Pruning and wiring It does not take to severe pruning of the root system, so this needs to be gradual while selectively trimming the crown. If the reduction of the roots is fairly drastic, it is best to remove all the leaves. Cut back the new shoots to the first few leaves during growth. Carry out wiring from spring to autumn, protecting the bark of the younger branches.

Feeding Every 20–30 days from early spring to autumn, with an interval of a couple of months in midsummer.

Notes Remove all suckers from the base of the trunk and branches. Let the soil dry out partially between waterings. If the tree is growing strongly, the crown can be thickened by complete defoliation in spring every other year.

81 PITHECELLOBIUM DULCE Benth.

Introduction – see p. 101.

Repotting As for the majority of tropical plants, this operation is best carried out in the summer. Use sandy, well-drained soil and try not to disturb the roots too much, merely cutting back those which are winding around the inside of the pot or through the drainage holes. After repotting, keep the plant sheltered in a warm, bright place, avoiding direct exposure to sunlight; water frequently and spray the foliage. Repot every 2–3 years.

Pruning and wiring These operations should be done in summer. The plant can stand drastic pruning and forms strong scar tissue. Outside its native range it is advisable, however, to shorten the new shoots and trim the bigger branches only when essential. Bearing in mind that the branches tend to return to their original position and that the wood is fairly fragile, it is best to position the bigger branches gradually with ties.

Feeding Abundantly before and after the growing season. As with all tropical plants, it is advisable to fertilize as well during the winter.

Notes An indoor or hothouse plant. In the former case it is necessary to spray the foliage at least once a day and to keep the plant in a bright place.

82 PODOCARPUS NAGI Makino

A small tree, sometimes a shrub, from Japan, China, and Taiwan, which grows slowly and is quite long-lived. It has evergreen, leathery, flexible, lanceolate, and linear leaves, similar to those of the yew, but 1½–2 in (4–5 cm) long, dark green above, lighter below, and globose fruits.

Repotting Every 3–4 years in spring, using 50% soil, 20% peat, and 30% coarse sand.

Pruning and wiring Initial positional pruning of the roots should be done gradually while repotting and selectively reducing the crown. Shorten the new shoots in late spring when they are still tender. If necessary, repeat the operation in late summer. Positional wiring of the trunk and branches may be done at any time of year.

Feeding From spring to autumn, once a month. Administer chelated iron once or twice a year.

Notes A robust and sturdy tree, it can be kept indoors or outdoors. In the latter case it should be protected under glass in winter; in the former it is necessary to spray the foliage at least once daily and to expose the plant to sunlight in spring and summer.

83 PORTULACARIA AFRA Jacq.

A succulent plant originally from southern Africa, it has a gray-brown trunk and fleshy jade-green leaves. The pale pink flowers are in upright racemes.

Repotting Every 2–3 years in spring, with 40% soil and 60% coarse sand or equivalent material.

Pruning and wiring Reduce and position the roots while repotting and eliminate any branches not necessary for the final design. Shorten the new shoots at the beginning and end of summer. Although wiring is possible, it is better to shape the tree by pruning.

Feeding From spring to the end of summer at intervals of 30–40 days.

Notes Although it is debatable as to whether this is really a bonsai, it does present certain features which justify it being classified as such. At any rate it is a suitable indoor plant, to be kept in a bright position, the foliage sprayed periodically, and watered sparingly throughout the summer. In spring–summer expose it directly to sunlight. Keep a careful watch on any wiring, removing any pieces likely to cut into the bark.

84 POTENTILLA FRUTICOSA L.

A small shrub with deciduous, 5-lobed leaves and dark brown trunk with bark that flakes off. It has long-lasting, showy, bright yellow flowers in summer.

Repotting Every 2 years in spring, before the buds open, with 60% soil, 10% peat, and 30% coarse sand or equivalent material.

Pruning and wiring Carry out the initial root pruning at the same time as repotting. Shorten the new shoots in autumn, after flowering. Unwanted branches can be removed at any time. Carry out positional wiring of the trunk and branches from spring to autumn.

Feeding Once every 20–30 days from early to late spring and from the end of summer to late autumn.

Notes This plant is particularly used as a mame bonsai and valued both for its unusual leaf shape and for its long flowering period. Although it likes to live in bright places, it must be protected from direct and prolonged exposure to sunlight in summer, and the soil should not be allowed to dry out completely. Get rid of faded flowers after flowering and dried branches in spring.

85 PRUNUS ARMENIACA L.

The apricot is a medium-sized tree, originally ranging from Iran to Manchuria. Cultivated in the East from time immemorial, it was introduced to the Mediterranean area by the Romans. It has deciduous, petiolate, oval, and pointed leaves and pinkish-white flowers which appear on the branches before the leaves sprout. The fruit is the familiar apricot.

Repotting Every 2 years in early spring – or autumn in warmer climates – with 70% soil and 30% coarse sand or equivalent material.

Pruning and wiring Position and reduce the roots while repotting and selectively trimming the foliage. Leave a good root system and repeat the operation when next repotting. Cut back the new shoots after flowering in late spring. Position the trunk and branches from spring to summer, protecting the bark.

Feeding Once every 20 days from early spring to the end of autumn stopping for about a month during the hottest part of summer. Administer chelated iron a couple of times a year and, in autumn, use a fertilizer high in phosphorus and potassium.

Notes A fairly sturdy and adaptable tree, it must be protected, when in a bonsai pot, during the winter. Expose to full sun but avoid the soil completely drying out. Water generously in spring.

86 PRUNUS MAHALEB L.

A small tree or, more frequently, a shrub, the Saint Lucie cherry has a vast range extending from the Iberian peninsula to the Caucasus and western Asia. It has alternate, petiolate, deciduous leaves, oval with a short pointed tip and minutely toothed margins, bisexual white flowers in upright corymbs, and round drupes, blackish when ripe.

Repotting Every 2–3 years in spring or autumn, before the leaves appear or after they fall, with 60% soil, 10% peat, and 30% coarse sand.

Pruning and wiring The initial positional pruning of the roots should be carried out while repotting and selective reduction of the aerial part. Seal the wounds with a good sealing compound. Pinch out the still tender new shoots in spring, after flowering, or shorten them in late summer. Wire to position the trunk and branches from spring to summer, protecting the bark.

Feeding At least 3 months after repotting, every 20–30 days from early spring to the beginning of summer and from late summer to mid autumn. In the latter period use a fertilizer high in potassium and phosphorus.

Notes Get rid of unwanted suckers at the base of pruned branches and trunk. Be careful not to let the soil dry out completely.

87 **PRUNUS MUME** Sieb. et Zucc.

A small tree originally from China and Korea, with a dark gray trunk and young branches that are bright green. The leaves are deciduous, round or oval, with long pointed tips. The scented flowers are solitary or in pairs. Unusually, it flowers early, in January–February, before the leaves appear, according to climatic conditions; and the flowers range in color, from dark pink to white.

Repotting Every 1–2 years with 80% soil and 20% coarse sand or equivalent material.

Pruning and wiring Eliminate branches unnecessary to final design while repotting and reduce the root system at the same time, making sure it remains fairly compact. Shorten the new shoots before they harden throughout the growth period. Carry out wiring from spring to autumn, protecting the bark and proceeding cautiously because of the fragility of the branches. When possible, resort to other methods (ties, weights, etc.) to shape the tree.

Feeding Every 30 days from spring to autumn.

Notes Eliminate faded flowers immediately after flowering. Never allow the soil to dry out completely and water abundantly in spring. Do not expose the plant for too long to direct sunlight in summer. Protect under glass in winter.

---

88 **PRUNUS PERSICA** Batsch

The peach is a small tree or shrub, believed to come from China. Cultivated in that country for millennia, it is found throughout the Mediterranean area, having been introduced by the soldiers of Alexander the Great who discovered it in Persia. Today it is known in hundreds of varieties, both fruiting and flowering. The short-stalked leaves are deciduous, lanceolate and alternate, the trunk has smooth or slightly fissured bark, and the flowers are pink or red. The fruit is the familiar peach.

Repotting Every year at the end of winter, with 80% soil and 20% coarse sand.

Pruning and wiring Position and cut back the roots during the spring repotting. Prune the branches after flowering, sealing the cuts with a good sealing compound. Shorten the new shoots in early spring. Carry out positional pruning of the trunk and branches from spring to summer, protecting the bark.

Feeding Every 20–30 days, starting at least 3 months after repotting.

Notes When in a bonsai pot, the tree needs to be kept in full sun, but avoid direct and prolonged exposure in midsummer. Never allow the soil to dry out entirely. Protect during winter.

89 PSEUDOCYDONIA SINENSIS Scheid.

A small tree or shrub, originally from China, with purple-gray bark that flakes off in brownish-yellow strips when mature. The short-stalked leaves are deciduous, ovate with a blunt tip, the solitary flowers are light pink, and the golden-yellow fruits persist on the plant after the leaves fall. The species owes much of its popularity to bonsai.

Repotting Every 1–2 years in spring or autumn, with 60% soil, 10% peat, and 30% coarse sand or equivalent material.

Pruning and wiring Positional pruning of the roots can be done during the first repotting. Trim the unwanted branches in late spring, shortening them gradually over a couple of years. Reduce the new shoots from the end of spring to summer. Carry out wiring to position trunk and branches from early summer to autumn, protecting the bark.

Feeding Every 15–20 days during growth, beginning at least 3 months after repotting.

Notes See that the soil never dries out completely and spray the foliage from time to time in midsummer. During this period avoid exposing the tree for too long to direct sunlight.

90 PSEUDOLARIX AMABILIS Rehd.

A medium-sized, slow-growing tree originally from south-eastern China (Chekiang and Kiangsi). The bark is ash gray or gray-brown, fissured when mature, and the leaves are deciduous and flexible, jade green, similar to those of the larch but slightly bigger.

Repotting In early spring, before the buds open, with 60% soil, 10% peat, and 30% coarse sand; every 2–3 years for young specimens, every 3–5 years for older ones.

Pruning and wiring Initial positional pruning of the roots should be done while repotting. Prune the branches during the winter rest period. Shorten the new shoots, pinching them out when still tender or cutting them back in the winter to the first or second bud. Position the trunk and branches with wire in late summer to autumn.

Feeding Once every 20–30 days from early spring to autumn. Administer chelated iron a couple of times a year. To encourage the tree to lignify, feed with a potassium-rich fertilizer from late summer to autumn.

Notes Among larches, this one, the golden larch, is the most tolerant climatically. But because it is sensitive to large quantities of lime, use, when possible, rain water.

91 PUNICA GRANATUM L.

A small tree originating in Asia, the pomegranate is now a naturalized constituent of the Mediterranean flora. The short-stalked leaves are deciduous, simple, usually opposite, lanceolate and entire, with a blunt or pointed tip, the flowers are scarlet and the fruit is a round false-berry.

Repotting Every 1–2 years in spring, with 60% soil, 10% peat, and 30% coarse sand or equivalent material.

Pruning and wiring Initial pruning of the roots should be done during repotting and selective reduction of the foliage. Trim the crown in early spring or late summer. Wire from late spring to autumn, protecting the bark and proceeding carefully to avoid breaking the fragile branches.

Feeding Every 20–30 days from early spring to autumn. In the latter period use a complete fertilizer high in phosphorus and potassium.

Notes Avoid prolonged exposure to the sun in midsummer. The soil should never be allowed to dry out completely. It is essential to protect the plant under glass in winter.

---

92 PUNICA GRANATUM L. var. 'NANA'

This small shrub grows to no more than about 16 in (40 cm). The leaves, flowers, and fruits are similar to those of *P. granatum* but are very much smaller in size.

Repotting Every 1–2 years in early spring, before the buds open, with 70% soil and 30% coarse sand.

Pruning and wiring Cutting back of the root system should be done gradually during repottings. Prune the branches in early spring and shorten the shoots in late summer after the flowers fade. Wire in late spring to summer; protect the bark and proceed carefully because the bigger branches are rather fragile.

Feeding Every 15–20 days from spring to autumn, using ¼ of the dose recommended by the makers. Do not feed while flowering. In autumn use fertilizers high in phosphorus and potassium.

Notes This is a particularly suitable variety for bonsai. Eliminate any shoots at the base of the trunk and branches. Never let the soil dry out completely and keep the plant sheltered from end autumn to spring.

93 PYRACANTHA COCCINEA Roem.

An evergreen, thorny shrub, sometimes quite large, originally from southern Europe and western Asia. The leaves, with finely toothed margins, are glossy above and – when young – hairy below. The clusters of flowers are white or pinkish yellow, followed by many fruits which persist through the winter.

Repotting Every 2–3 years in spring, with 80% soil and 20% coarse sand or equivalent material.

Pruning and wiring Initial positional pruning of the roots should be carried out at the same time as repotting and selective reduction of the crown; always leave a good root system and repeat the operation at the next repotting. Reduce the new shoots while still tender during the entire growing season and shorten the smaller branches in autumn. Wire to position trunk and branches from spring to summer.

Feeding Once every 20–30 days from spring to autumn.

Notes The shrub is normally very sturdy in the wild but when grown as a bonsai needs protection in winter. Keep in full sun but never allow the soil to dry out completely.

94 PYRUS PYRASTER Burgsd.

A tree which may grow to a height of 50 ft (15 m) but is often a shrub, with thorny branches, originally from central-eastern Europe and Asia Minor. The long-stalked leaves are deciduous, alternate, simple, ovate with finely toothed margins, dark green above and paler green below. The white flowers, in erect corymbs, are bisexual, the fruits are long pomes. The wild form is considered to be the ancestor of numerous cultivars of pear.

Repotting Every 1–2 years in early spring or autumn, with 50% soil, 20% peat, and 30% coarse sand.

Pruning and wiring Carry out initial pruning of the roots when repotting at the same time as selective reduction of the crown. Shorten the new shoots to the first leaves in late spring–early summer. Position the trunk and branches with wire from summer to autumn.

Feeding Once a month from spring to autumn with ¼ the dose recommended by the makers. In autumn use fertilizers with a high concentration of phosphorus and potassium.

Notes This tree can withstand quite drastic treatment of the roots. Eliminate all suckers at the base of the trunk, on the branches, and at the edges of the scar callus resulting from pruning. Once in the bonsai container, protect the roots in winter.

95 QUERCUS ILEX L.

The holly oak is a very long-lived tree or shrub which grows all around the Mediterranean, notably near the coast at an altitude of about 5,000 ft (1,500 m). The leaves are persistent, simple, alternate, short-stalked, ovate-oblong with entire or dentate-mucronate margins, the upper surface smooth, glossy and dark green, the underside downy and gray-green. The flowers are monoecious, the fruits are nuts (acorns), partially protected by a hemispherical cup.

Repotting Every 2–3 years in late spring, with 60% soil, 10% peat, and 30% coarse sand or equivalent material.

Pruning and wiring Cut back the tap-root periodically during repotting. If done drastically it is advisable, in order to stimulate rooting, to remove all the leaves. Prune the branches in spring, before the new growth cycle, and shorten the new shoots from spring to autumn, leaving a pair of leaves. Wire from spring to autumn, protecting the bark of the larger branches.

Feeding Every 30 days from early spring to the beginning of summer and from late summer to late autumn.

Notes Keep in full sun but avoid letting the soil dry out entirely. Protect during winter.

96 QUERCUS ROBUR L.

The English oak is a long-lived tree that grows over a vast area comprising Europe, the Caucasus, and Asia Minor. The bark is gray-black, deeply furrowed at maturity; the short-stalked leaves are alternate and deciduous, with 3–6 pairs of wavy surfaced lobes, blunt at the margins, dark green above and pale green below. The flowers are monoecious, the fruits are nuts (acorns), partially protected by a hemispherical cup.

Repotting Every 2–3 years in spring, when the buds open, with 60% soil, 10% peat, and 30% coarse sand or equivalent material.

Pruning and wiring Shorten the tap-root gradually during repotting, always leaving a good root system. Reduce the crown selectively when first repotting, discarding branches not necessary to the final design. Cut back the shoots during growth when still tender. Position the trunk and branches in late spring and summer.

Feeding Once a month from early spring to early summer and from the end of summer to late autumn.

Notes Eliminate undesirable suckers at the base of the trunk or around the scars on pruned branches.

(See also notes on *Q. suber.*)

97 QUERCUS SUBER L.

The cork oak is a medium-sized tree with typically thick, suberose bark, its original range covering the Iberian peninsula, Dalmatia and northwest Africa. The leaves are persistent, alternate, and simple, with a pointed tip, dark green above and gray-green below. The fruit is a nut (acorn), partially protected by a hemispherical cup.

Repotting Every 2–3 years in spring, when the buds open, with 60% soil and 40% coarse sand.

Pruning and wiring Cut back the tap-root gradually at each repotting, always leaving a good root system. Eventually all the leaves can be removed. Shorten the new shoots during the growth period. Carry out wiring from spring to autumn, protecting the bark.

Feeding Once every 20–30 days in spring and autumn.
Notes Protect during winter.

98 RHODODENDRON INDICUM Sweet

The Setsuki azalea is an evergreen shrub, originally from Japan, which can grow to a height of about 6 ft (2 m). The flowers – which can be of different colors on the same plant – may be pinkish white, pink, reddish or white, single or in pairs. There are some 700 different cultivars and it is one of the most common plants used as a bonsai.

Repotting In late spring after flowering, every 2–3 years, with acidic soil. It is advisable to use specific potting mixtures specially prepared for azaleas and rhododendrons.

Pruning and wiring Shorten the roots while repotting, prune the branches and the new shoots in late summer, sealing the cuts with a good sealing compound. Position the trunk and branches from spring to summer, proceeding with care because the main branches are brittle. Do not water on the day preceding the wiring, so that branches will bend more easily.

Feeding Plants repotted in spring should not be fertilized until autumn. Otherwise, feed once every 20–30 days from early spring to late autumn, stopping for about a month during the hottest part of summer. Administer chelated iron a couple of times a year.
Notes Never allow the soil to dry out completely and protect under glass in winter. In spring and summer avoid exposing to direct and prolonged sun. Apply rain water. If tap water is high in lime, repot every year.

99 RHUS COTINUS L.
Cotinus coggygria Scop.

This shrub, originally from central and southern Europe, rarely takes the form of a tree. The bark is reddish brown, initially smooth, fissured when mature, with short-stalked, deciduous, alternate, oval leaves, normally light green with some assuming a lovely coral red color in autumn. The typical abundant, feathery panicles of fruit stalks covered with long hairs explain why it is sometimes called the smoke tree. The fruits are small reddish drupes.

Repotting In spring, before the buds open, with 60% soil and 40% coarse sand or equivalent material.

Pruning and wiring Major pruning of the root system should coincide with repotting and selective reduction of the aerial part. The branches can be shortened in the growing season, but leave a few strong lateral branches. Reduce the new shoots after flowering.

Feeding Once a month in spring and autumn.

Notes Because the branches are delicate it is best, if possible, to shape the tree by pruning and to carry out wiring in spring with the utmost care and patience. Allow the soil to dry out partially between successive applications of water. Eliminate undesirable suckers at the base of the trunk or from pruned branches. Protect under glass in winter.

100 RIBES UVA-CRISPA L.

The gooseberry is a thorny shrub with grayish stem and branches, originally from central and northern Europe. It grows to a height of 2–5 ft (60–150 cm). The leaves are simple with 3–5 dentate lobes and stem from the axil of the tripartite spines. The 1–3 green or reddish flowers are borne in racemes. The fruits are oval berries, a little larger than a pea in wild species.

Repotting Once a year in spring, before the leaves appear, with 60% soil, 10% peat, and 30% coarse sand.

Pruning and wiring Initial pruning to position the roots should be done while repotting and selectively reducing the crown. Shorten the new shoots after flowering and before they harden. Wiring to position the trunk and branches can be done at any time of year.

Feeding Once a month in spring to late autumn, stopping for about a month during the hottest part of summer. In the latter period use a fertilizer high in phosphorus and potassium.

Notes The shrub is customarily used as a mame and will tolerate poorish light, although ideally it should be placed in bright light during autumn and winter and semi-shade in spring and summer. Do not allow the soil to dry out completely.

101 ROSMARINUS OFFICINALIS L.

An evergreen shrub found throughout the Mediterranean region. The trunk is light brown and scaly, the leaves are sessile, lanceolate, and slightly revolute, rough on the upper side, whitish and downy on the underside. The flowers are usually pale blue, arranged in axillary racemes.

Repotting Early spring or end of summer, with 60% soil and 40% coarse sand or equivalent material.

Pruning and wiring Position the root system while repotting, at the same time getting rid of any branches unnecessary to the final design. To thicken the foliage, pinch out new shoots with the nails throughout the growing season or cut them back in early autumn. Position the trunk and branches with wire from spring to summer.

Feeding Once a month in spring and autumn.

Notes This shrub is especially popular for its trunk and its long flowering period. It responds well to pruning but may encounter some difficulties in the initial repottings. To encourage rooting, keep the shrub in bright but indirect light after covering it with a plastic sheet, or keep it in a bright greenhouse, watering plentifully and spraying the foliage several times a day. Normally water is needed only when the soil partially dries out. Protect in winter.

102 SAGERETIA THEA M. C. Johnst.

A shrub or small tree, originally from central-southern China, with brown bark which flakes off in pale strips, oval, alternate, short-stalked leaves, small pinkish-white flowers and dark red fruits.

Repotting Every 2–3 years in spring, when temperatures are higher than 54°F (12°C), using 60% soil, 10% peat, and 30% coarse sand.

Pruning and wiring Prune the root system while repotting, at the same time reducing or eliminating branches not necessary to the plant's final design. Outside its native range it is best merely to shorten the larger roots and those growing out of the pot. Reduce the shoots to the first leaves during growth. Position the trunk and branches with wire from spring to summer, at least 3 months after repotting.

Feeding Once every 20–30 days from spring to summer and from the end of summer to late autumn.

Notes It is one of the sturdiest tropical plants, to be kept both indoors and outdoors. In the latter case it must be protected under glass in winter. Water generously and, when indoors, spray the foliage at least once daily.

103   SALIX ALBA L. var. 'TRISTIS' Gaud.

This cultivar from *S. alba* (white willow) and *S. babylonica* (*Chinese weeping willow*) possesses the best qualities of both species. It is a tree of medium size, with drooping branches and lovely golden-yellow twigs. The leaves are deciduous, lanceolate and alternate, and the male and female flower catkins are usually present on the same plant but occasionally on different ones.

Repotting Every 2–3 years in spring, with 60% soil, 20% peat, and 20% coarse sand.

Pruning and wiring Cut back the roots while repotting and at the same time get rid of branches not necessary to the final design. Shorten unwanted new shoots in late autumn. Wiring may be done from spring to summer, protecting the bark. Good results can also be obtained with weights which cause the branches to bend.

Feeding At least 3 months after repotting, every 20–30 days from early spring to late autumn, stopping during the hottest part of summer.

Notes Reasonable results can be achieved in a few years by complying with the natural weeping habit of the tree, which should be grown with pendulous branches. The soil must never be allowed to dry out completely and during summer a bowl of water underneath will help the tree get the necessary moisture.

---

104   SCHEFFLERA ACTINOPHYLLA Harms

The plant comes from Australia, New Guinea, Java, and the Pacific islands, and in these places it may grow to a height of about 100 ft (30 m). The leaves are palmate-compound with 5–7 oval segments. The flowers, in terminal racemes, are dark red and the fruits are red. The most commonly used variety as a bonsai is "Chisae."

Repotting Every 2 years in spring, with 60% soil and 40% coarse sand.

Pruning and wiring While repotting shorten the trunks to the first leaves. During growth remove the bigger leaves. Wiring to position the trunks is not usually necessary but possible in summer.

Feeding Once a month.

Notes If planted on a rock, keep the volcanic, porous rock constantly wet. If planted in a pot, water only when the soil is partially dried out. The ideal temperature is around 72°F (22°C), which should never be allowed to drop below 54°F (12°C). It tolerates poor light but will benefit from good exposure.

105   SCOLOPIA CHINENSIS Hook. f.

A small thorny evergreen tree or shrub, distributed over an area comprising Southeast Asia, southern China, and Taiwan, with a light gray-brown, slightly fissured trunk. The leaves are whorled, oval, with a short pointed tip, the yellowish-white flowers are bisexual, in fairly small axillary racemes, and the fleshy berries are reddish.

Repotting Every 2–3 years in late spring, with 50% soil, 20% peat, and 30% coarse sand.

Pruning and wiring Outside its native range it is best, while repotting, merely to shorten the roots that have formed around the container and above the drainage holes, at the same time pruning unwanted branches and shortening the others. During the growth period pinch out the new shoots when still tender. Wire from spring to autumn.

Feeding Once a month from early spring to summer and in autumn. Use a fertilizer high in phosphorus and potassium during autumn.

Notes The tree does well indoors but should be placed in a very bright position and exposed to direct sunlight in summer. Never allow the soil to dry out completely and spray the foliage at least once a day. Avoid sudden changes of temperature.

106   SEMIARUNDINARIA FASTUOSA Mak. ex Nakai

This bamboo is originally from Japan, where it forms dense clumps of dark green canes, up to 50 ft (15 m) high. The leaves are evergreen and lanceolate. The growth of bamboos is faster than that of other plants so a bamboo bonsai needs careful treatment. For an understanding of their growth processes, consult a book on bamboo.

Repotting Every 2–3 years in late spring, with 60% soil, 20% peat, and 20% coarse sand or equivalent material.

Pruning and wiring Because these plants are generally used to create clumps, the arrangement of the roots (rhizomes) is a determining factor. During repotting get rid of any trunks that are too long or in a bad position. To arrest the trunks at the required height, simply remove the center of the new shoots before they open. This operation, continued throughout the growing season, will help control the shape of the composition at all times.

Feeding Once a month from spring to autumn.

Notes The plant needs continual watering and foliage spraying, particularly in hot weather. Avoid direct and prolonged exposure to sunlight. Protect in winter.

107 SEQUOIADENDRON GIGANTEUM Buchh. 'PYGMAEUM'

This dwarf cultivar of one of the tallest trees in the world has squamiform leaves arranged in spirals around the branches, on which they persist for more than 4 years. It is a very long-lived conifer.

Repotting In early spring, every 3–5 years, with 70% soil and 30% coarse sand or equivalent material.

Pruning and wiring Carry out positional pruning of the roots gradually during first repottings and on these occasions eliminate branches not necessary to the final design of the plant. Pinch out tender new shoots during growth. Position the trunk and branches with wire from spring to autumn, but at least one complete growth cycle after repotting. Because the branches snap easily at the trunk, it is necessary to proceed gradually and carefully.

Feeding Once ever 30 days during spring and autumn.

Notes A stiff tree, there may be difficulties in shaping the crown. Eliminate unwanted suckers at the base of the branches and never let the soil dry out completely.

108 SERISSA FOETIDA Lam.

This small shrub from Southeast Asia owes its name to the disagreeable smell given out both by the leaves when rubbed and the roots when cut. The small oval leaves are evergreen and opposite, the flowers white and solitary. There are varieties with double flowers and variegated foliage.

Repotting Every 2–3 years in late spring, with 50% soil, 20% peat, and 30% coarse sand.

Pruning and wiring Shorten the roots during repotting and get rid of unwanted branches. Position the trunk and branches from late spring to autumn, preferably in the latter season. Protect the bark from any wiring which entails a major change in the direction of branches or trunk.

Feeding Once every 20–30 days from spring to autumn and a couple of times from autumn to spring.

Notes This is an indoor bonsai which can be kept outdoors in late spring and summer. Avoid sudden changes of temperature as well as direct and prolonged exposure to sunlight. Keep the soil constantly moist. Remove faded flowers and shoots from the base of trunk and roots.

109 SPIRAEA JAPONICA L. f.

A shrub with deciduous leaves growing over a vast area including China, the Himalayas, Korea, and Japan. The short-stalked leaves are lanceolate and oval, with finely toothed margins, and the flowers, in terminal corymbs, are pink.

Repotting Every 1–2 years in early spring, with 80% soil and 20% coarse sand.

Pruning and wiring Position the roots during the initial repotting, at the same time removing branches not necessary to the final design of the plant. Shorten the new shoots in autumn and remove those forming at the base of the branches. Wiring, although not necessary, can be done from spring to summer. Shaping of the crown is normally effected by periodic pruning.

Feeding Once every 20 days in spring and autumn, but beginning at least 2 months after repotting.

Notes Interesting mainly for its lovely flowers, the shrub is generally used as a mame, often in roots-on-rock style. Never let the soil dry out entirely and protect in winter.

110 SYRINGA MICROPHYLLA Diels.

A small shrub originally from northwest China, with small, slightly pointed oval leaves and flowers in terminal panicles, dark violet-pink outside, lighter inside. In nature the plant never grows to more than about 6 ft (2 m).

Repotting Every year in early spring, before the buds open, using 70% soil and 30% coarse sand or equivalent material.

Pruning and wiring The initial drastic work on the roots should be done at the same time as repotting and selective reduction of the foliage. Shorten the new shoots in autumn. Wire for positioning of the trunk and branches from spring to autumn.

Feeding Once every 20 days beginning after flowering and continuing until autumn. Do not fertilize for at least 3 months after repotting. Use a fertilizer high in phosphorus and potassium in autumn.

Notes Keep the soil constantly moist during the growing period and reduce watering in autumn and winter. Spray the foliage in midsummer. Remove fading flowers as well as suckers at the base of the trunk.

111　TAMARINDUS INDICA L.

An Asian tree of uncertain origin, the tamarind is evergreen with thin, rough, blackish bark. The leaves are alternate, leathery, pinnate with tiny leaflets. The pale yellow flowers are in racemes and the fruit is a legume.

Repotting In spring, every 2–3 years, with 70% soil and 30% coarse sand or equivalent material.

Pruning and wiring Remove and prune roots encircling the pot and above the drainage holes during repotting. At the same time get rid of any branches not necessary to the plant's final design. Outside its range it is best to let the new shoots develop and to shape the crown by cutting back in late summer. Wire from late spring to summer.

Feeding Once a month from spring to autumn. Do not fertilize for at least 3 months after repotting.

Notes The tree can be kept indoors or in the greenhouse. If indoors, put it in a bright position, spraying the foliage often. In summer expose it directly to the sun. Allow the soil to dry out slightly between waterings.

112　TAMARIX CHINENSIS Lour.

A tall tree or small shrub from northern China and Manchuria. The bark is brown and fissured, the twigs are dark red, the leaves are deciduous, feathery, lanceolate, keeled and pale green, and the small, pink flowers are in racemes which develop on the current year's growth.

Repotting Every 2–3 years in spring, before the leaves appear, with 60% soil, 20% peat, and 20% coarse sand.

Pruning and wiring Drastic pruning of the roots can be done to coincide with repotting and the selective reduction of the aerial part. Prune the new shoots in autumn, but during growth limit this to removing unwanted shoots. Carry out wiring from spring to autumn, protecting the bark.

Feeding From spring to autumn, every 30 days, with a gap in the summer. In autumn apply a fertilizer high in phosphorus and potassium.

Notes This is a sturdy and adaptable tree. To get an attractive effect, make sure the branches hang down by means of repeated wiring and pruning. Always keep the soil moist, even in winter, and protect under glass in the coldest weather.

113   **TAXODIUM DISTICHUM** Rich.

The bald cypress is a deciduous conifer from the southern United States, with a pyramidal habit. The bark is reddish brown, and the soft pale green leaves are alternate, needle-like and arranged in two rows. The fruit is a small cone.

Repotting Every 2–3 years, in autumn or spring, with 80% soil and 20% coarse sand or equivalent material.

Pruning and wiring Prune the roots while repotting – preferably in autumn – at the same time selectively reducing the crown. Shorten the new shoots by pinching them out with the fingers during the entire period of growth, before they harden. Wire to position the trunk and branches from spring to summer; keep careful watch and remove the wire before it starts cutting into the bark.

Feeding Every 20–30 days from spring to autumn, stopping during the hottest part of summer.

Notes Expose to full sun but avoid letting the soil dry out completely. Place the pot in a saucer of water in summer so that the roots can absorb water constantly. Do not wire the branches for at least 3 months after repotting. Remove unwanted suckers along the trunk and branches. Protect during winter.

114   **TAXUS BACCATA** L.

A slow-growing dioecious tree, evergreen and long-lived, the yew is distributed over Europe, North Africa, and Asia Minor. The thin bark flakes off when mature. The leaves, in two rows, are linear and pointed, the upper surface shiny dark green, the underside light green with two horizontal stomatal bands.

Repotting In spring, every 2–3 years for young specimens, every 3–5 years for older ones, with 60% soil, 10% peat, and 30% coarse sand.

Pruning and wiring Cut back the roots in stages during repottings, always leaving a good root system. Prune the branches in autumn–winter. *Jin* and *Shari* can be created during the growing season (spring–summer). Pinch out the tender new shoots during growth. Wiring to position the trunk and branches can be done at any time, but preferably at the end of winter or in autumn.

Feeding Once a month in spring and autumn.

Notes This tree is a slow grower and particularly suitable for all the styles entailing the use of dry wood. Despite its resistance to cold, when potted as a bonsai the roots need protection in winter. Choose female seed-bearing trees because the bright red fruits are an attractive feature in winter.

115 **TAXUS CUSPIDATA** Sieb. et Zucc.

Originally from Japan, Korea, and Manchuria, this plant differs from *T. baccata* in having sickle-shaped leaves distinguished by a dark, mucronulate tip. It is fairly long-lived and slow-growing.

Repotting Every 3–5 years, depending on the plant's age, in spring, with 60% soil, 10% peat, and 30% coarse sand or equivalent material.

Pruning and wiring Position the roots while repotting and selectively reducing the crown. Proceed gradually, always leaving a good root system. Pinch out the new shoots when still tender, during the entire growth period. Further pruning of the branches can be done in spring or autumn. Position the trunk and branches with wire from autumn to spring, but before the buds open.

Feeding Every 20–30 days in spring and autumn. Do not fertilize for 3–4 months after repotting.

Notes Do not water excessively but never allow the soil to dry out completely. Keep in semi-shade during spring–summer. Spray the foliage periodically.

116 **THYMUS VULGARIS** L.

A small shrub with twisted branches, growing to a height of about 12 in (30 cm), along the coastal Mediterranean regions. The stem is woody with bark that flakes off in thin strips; the small leaves are evergreen, linear, downy above, whitish beneath. The flowers are white to lilac.

Repotting Every 2–3 years in early spring, with 60% soil and 40% coarse sand.

Pruning and wiring Shorten the roots while repotting, always leaving a good root system. At the same time remove any branches not necessary to the final design, and shorten the other branches, leaving some vegetation. Shorten the new shoots after flowering. Wiring – not usually necessary because the plant is best shaped by pruning – can be done from spring to autumn.

Feeding Once a month in spring and autumn. Apply a fertilizer high in phosphorus and potassium in autumn.

Notes This tree is very suitable for creating mame bonsai, but there may be some difficulty in rooting after repotting.

117 TILIA CORDATA Miller

A medium-sized tree, the littleleaf linden (small leaved lime) has a vast range including much of Europe. The trunk is smooth, becoming blackish and fissured when mature. The leaves are alternate, simple, petiolate, and cordate with finely toothed margins. The scented, bisexual flowers are in cymes and the small, nut-like fruits are covered by a leafy bract.

Repotting In early spring, before the buds open, with 70% soil, 10% peat, and 20% coarse sand; every 1–2 years for young plants, every 2–3 years for older ones.

Pruning and wiring Major pruning of the roots can be done when repotting. Eliminate or shorten branches in autumn; in the latter instance always leave a few buds. Pinch out the tender new shoots during the growing period. Wire from spring to the end of summer, making sure to protect the bark of the branches and the young plants.

Feeding Every 20–30 days in spring and autumn.

Notes With healthy trees it is possible to reduce the size of the leaves by defoliating in the first half of June. Leave the stalk and water sparingly until the new, smaller leaves are completely formed.

118 TSUGA CANADENSIS Carr. 'MINIMA'

This is one of the many cultivars of the eastern hemlock, slow growing, with drooping branches, a gray-brown trunk and small, flat, needles, gray-green above and paler below, with two horizontal stomatic bands.

Repotting Every 3–5 years in early spring, with 50% soil, 20% peat, and 30% coarse sand or equivalent material.

Pruning and wiring Cut back the roots gradually, in stages while repotting and at the same time remove unnecessary branches. Cover the cuts with a good sealing compound and take care not to detach large pieces of bark. Pinch out the strongest shoots with the fingers, removing three quarters during the growing season. Position the trunk and branches with wire from autumn to spring.

Feeding Once a month in spring and autumn. Administer chelated iron 2–3 times a year.

Notes This a very suitable plant for creating mame. It has to be protected in summer from direct sunlight and in winter from possible frosts. Never allow the soil to dry out completely and spray the foliage with water from time to time in the hottest weather.

119 TSUGA DIVERSIFOLIA Mast.

This medium-sized evergreen tree from central and northern Japan has orange-brown bark, scaly when mature, and flat needles almost always arranged in opposite rows, dark green on the upper surface, lighter green on the underside, with two horizontal white stomatal bands.

Repotting Every 3–5 years, in early spring, with 50% soil, 20% peat, and 30% coarse sand.

Pruning and wiring Shorten the roots gradually and in stages while repotting. At the same time remove branches not necessary to the final design. Pinch out the new shoots throughout the growing season. Wiring may be done at any time except in spring.

Feeding Once a month in spring and autumn. Apply chelated iron a couple of times a year.

Notes Never allow the soil to dry out entirely and do not expose to full sun in midsummer. Do not prune drastically. Use rain water or water that has been standing for a while. If the water happens to contain a good deal of lime, repot more frequently.

120 ULMUS PARVIFOLIA Jacq.

A medium-sized tree, originally from central and northern China, Korea, and Japan. The Chinese elm has grayish bark that flakes off in rounded plates when mature, and small, short-stalked leaves, oval with a pointed tip and toothed margins, bright green on the upper surface, lighter green underneath.

Repotting In early spring or autumn, with 70% soil and 30% coarse sand.

Pruning and wiring Drastic positional pruning of the roots may be done while repotting, together with selective reduction of the crown. Shorten the new shoots during growth by pinching them out when still tender or by pruning them in summer. Wire from late spring to summer.

Feeding Once every 20–30 days from early spring to the beginning of summer, and in autumn.

Notes A semi-evergreen tree, it behaves as a deciduous species in cold-temperate climates. Virtually immune to disease, it is perhaps the strongest and most vigorous of bonsai subjects but needs continual pruning to maintain its shape in the growing season. Water only when the soil becomes partially dry.

121 VITEX NEGUNDO L.

A shrub originally from China and India with light brown bark, fissured when mature, and compound leaves of 3–5 parted, petiolate, oval-lanceolate leaflets. The violet-blue flowers are in upright terminal spikes.

Repotting Every 2–3 years in spring, before the buds open, with 60% soil, 20% peat, and 20% coarse sand or equivalent material.

Pruning and wiring Pruning of the root system should be done when repotting and cutting back the foliage. Outside its range it is best simply to shorten the roots that have grown around the pot and above the drainage holes. Prune the new shoots in late summer and cut back the branches in autumn after leaf fall. Wire to position the trunk and branches from spring to summer.

Feeding Once every 20–30 days in spring and autumn. In autumn use a fertilizer high in phosphorus and potassium.

Notes An indoor or greenhouse tree, it benefits from direct exposure to sunlight in midsummer. Never let the soil dry out completely.

122 WISTERIA FLORIBUNDA DC.

This climbing plant from Japan has a trunk which is usually twisted in a counter-clockwise direction. The leaves are imparipinnate, made up of 13–19 oval, deciduous leaflets. The usually scented violet-blue flowers are in long pendulous racemes and the pods are downy. Flower color ranges from violet through pink and white in the many cultivars.

Repotting Every 1–2 years in early spring or autumn, with 50% soil, 30% peat, and 20% coarse sand.

Pruning and wiring Position the roots during repottings, always leaving a good root mass. Shorten the shoots in late winter before buds begin to swell. Position the trunk and branches with wire after flowering.

Feeding Do not fertilize repotted plants for at least 2 months, then once every 15 days from early spring to time of flowering, continuing every 30 days until autumn and stopping in midsummer. In autumn use a fertilizer high in phosphorus and potassium.

Notes Expose to full sunlight and water abundantly during the growing season. In midsummer it is best to place the bonsai pot in a saucer so that the roots can take up sufficient water during the day, but do not let it stagnate.

123 ZELKOVA CARPINIFOLIA K. Koch

This tree from the Caucasus usually has a fairly short trunk and horizontal ascending branches. The bark is initially smooth and light gray, but when mature it flakes off in orange-yellow scales. The leaves are simple, oval with a pointed tip, toothed at the margins, the upper surface being dark green and the underside light green and hairy. There are inconspicuous male and female flowers on the same plant in clusters on the current year's shoots.

Repotting Every 1–2 years for young specimens, every 2–3 years for older ones, with 60% soil, 20% peat, and 20% coarse sand or equivalent material.

Pruning and wiring Prune the roots while repotting and at the same time eliminate branches not essential to the final design of the plant. Shorten the new shoots during the growing season by pinching out before they harden, or by cutting them back at the end of this period. Wiring can be done at any time of year, except spring.

Feeding Once every 20–30 days in spring and autumn.

Notes Never allow the soil to dry out entirely. Remove dead twigs at the end of winter and any suckers from the base of the branches during growth.

124 ZELKOVA SERRATA Mak.

This tree, originally from Japan, has smooth, gray bark. The leaves are deciduous, pointed, with toothed margins, the upper surface being dark green, the underside light green. The flowers are similar to those of *Z. carpinifolia*, and the fruits are drupes.

Repotting Every 2–3 years in early spring, with 60% soil, 20% peat, and 20% coarse sand. Plants cultivated in a very shallow bonsai container should be repotted every 1–2 years.

Pruning and wiring Prune the roots during repotting and the branches at the same time or in winter. Shorten the new shoots when still tender by pinching out with the fingers, or by cutting them back in late summer or autumn. Shaping of the tree is best effected by pruning the branches selectively. It is nevertheless possible to wire from spring to autumn.

Feeding Once every 20–30 days in spring and late summer to mid autumn.

Notes Keep in full sun but avoid exposing it for too long in midsummer, especially if the tree is in a very shallow container. Allow the soil to dry out slightly between waterings.

MEASUREMENTS AND SOURCES

Sources: C Coll. Günther Ruhe, Cassano Spinola; **Feb** Coll. Elio Boni, Florence; **Ffb** Coll. Francesco Birardi, Florence; **Fg** Coll. GianFranco Giorgi, Florence; **Fmb** Coll. Mauro Bini, Florence; **Fnz** Coll. Nicola Zannotti, Florence; **H** Bonsai Centrum, Heidelberg; **L** Coll. Andrea Niccolai, Lucca; **Pa** Centro Bonsai Crespi, Parabiago; **PC** Private Collection; **Pe** Centro Bonsai Franchi, Pescia; **Pi** Coll. Danilo Bonacchi, Pistoia; **Ta** Coll. Guido Degli'Innocenti, Tavarnuzze; **Tlv** Coll. Luciano Viaro, Triest; **Tms** Coll. Mario Starace, Triest.

page/ Entry	common name	botanical name	height	source
p. 2	Chinese elm	*Ulmus parvifolia*	24½ in (62 cm)	**Fg**
p. 10	trident maple	*Acer buergerianum*	13 in (33 cm)	**H**
p. 11	Japanese sago palm	*Cycas revoluta*	30 in (76 cm)	**Pe**
p. 20	*Penjing*		16½ in (42 cm)	**H**
p. 21	*Penjin*		15 in (38 cm)	**H**
p. 28	Chinese elm	*Ulmus parvifolia*	41¾ in (106 cm)	**Pe**
p. 29 a	orange jasmine	*Murraya paniculata*	38½ in (98 cm)	**H**
p. 29 b	rhododendron	*Rhododendron laterianum*	17¾ in (45 cm)	**H**
p. 38/39	mountain pine	*Pinus montana*	11¼ in (28 cm)	**Fg**
p. 47	Norway spruce	*Picea abies*	19¼ in (49 cm)	**Fg**
p. 48	needle juniper	*Juniperus rigida*	24½ in (62 cm)	**Pa**
p. 62	Japanese maple	*Acer palmatum*	19 in (48 cm)	**H**
p. 63	juniper	*Juniperus* sp.	28½ in (72 cm)	**H**
p. 64 l	Chinese elm	*Ulmus parvifolia*	4¼ in (12 cm)	**Fg**
p. 64 r	mastic tree	*Pistacia lentiscus*	2 in (5 cm)	**Fg**
p. 65	Yezo spruce	*Picea jezoensis*	36¼ in (92 cm)	**H**
p. 66	needle juniper	*Juniperus rigida*	23½ in (60 cm)	**H**
p. 67	mountain pine	*Pinus montana*	13¾ in (35 cm)	**C**
p. 68	Chinese elm	*Ulmus parvifolia*	26 in (66 cm)	**Pe**
p. 69	Chinese juniper	*Juniperus sargentii*	23½ in (60 cm)	**H**
p. 73	Japanese hornbeam	*Carpinus laxiflora*	19 in (48 cm)	**Pe**
p. 75	Zelkova	*Zelkova serrata*	25 in (64 cm)	**Pa**
p. 76/77	*Penjing*			**H**
p. 116/117	downy oak	*Quercus pubescens*	34 in (86 cm)	**Fg**
Entry 1	Nebrodi silver fir	*Abies nebrodensis*	13¾ in (35 cm)	**Fmb**
2	acacia	*Acacia* sp.	25½ in (65 cm)	**H**
3	trident maple	*Acer buergerianum*	17¾ in (45 cm)	**Pe**
4	field maple	*Acer campestre*	39½ in (100 cm)	**C**
5	Montpelier maple	*Acer monspessulanum*	19¼ in (49 cm)	**Fg**
6	Japanese maple	*Acer palmatum*	22 in (56 cm)	**Pe**
7	sycamore	*Acer pseudoplatanus*	17 in (43 cm)	**Fmb**
8	common horse chestnut	*Aesculus hippocastanum*	23¼ in (59 cm)	**H**
9	Italian alder	*Alnus cordata*	9½ in (24 cm)	**Fmb**
10	strawberry tree	*Arbustus unedo*	17¼ in (44 cm)	**Fg**
11	European white birch	*Betula verrucosa*	36¼ in (92 cm)	**C**
12	bougainvillea	*Bougainvillea glabra*	26½ in (67 cm)	**Pe**
13	box	*Buxus harlandii*	18 in (46 cm)	**Pe**
14	camellia	*Camellia japonica*	25½ in (65 cm)	**H**

15	hornbeam	*Carpinus betulus*	32 in (81 cm)	**Pe**
16	Japanese hornbeam	*Carpinus laxiflora*	26½ in (67 cm)	**H**
17	sweet chestnut	*Caslanea sativa*	33½ in (85 cm)	**Fg**
18	cedar of Lebanon	*Cedrus libani*	19 in (48 cm)	**Pe**
19	southern nettle-tree	*Celtis australis*	31½ in (80 cm)	**C**
20	Chinese nettle tree	*Celtis sinensis*	32¾ in (83 cm)	**H**
21	Judas tree, red bud	*Cercis silquastrum*	34½ in (88 cm)	**H**
22	flowering quince	*Chaenomeles speciosa*	14¼ in (36 cm)	**H**
23	hinoki cypress	*Chamaecyparis obtusa*	24½ in (62 cm)	**Pe**
24	hazel	*Corylus avellana* var. 'contorta'	24 in (61 cm)	**Fmb**
25	hawthorn	*Crataegus cuneata*	25 in (64 cm)	**H**
26	Japanese red cedar	*Cryptomeria japonica*	12½ in (32 cm)	**C**
27	Italian cypress	*Cupressus sempervirens*	26¾ in (68 cm)	**Pe**
28	Japanese sago palm	*Cycas revoluta*	25 in (64 cm)	**H**
29	quince	*Cydonia oblonga*	24½ in (62 cm)	**C**
30	pink, carnation	*Dianthus carthusianorum*	1 in (2.5 cm)	**Fg**
31	Chinese persimmon	*Diospyros kaki*	30¼ in (77 cm)	**Fmb**
32	carmona	*Ehretia microphilla*	8¼ in (21 cm)	**C**
33	oleaster	*Elaeagnus multiflora*	17¼ in (44 cm)	**Pe**
34	winged spindle	*Euonymus alatus*	10¼ in (26 cm)	**H**
35	milkweed	*Euphorbia balsamiphera*	16 in (41 cm)	**H**
36	Japanese blume	*Fagus crenata*	16½ in (42 cm)	**Feb**
37	European beech	*Fagus sylvatica*	19¾ in (50 cm)	**H**
38	weeping fig	*Figus benjamina*	42½ in (108 cm)	**H**
39	common fig	*Ficus carica*	21¾ in (55 cm)	**Pe**
40	fig	*Ficus neriifolia*	21¾ in (55 cm)	**H**
41	bo tree	*Ficus religiosa*	30¼ in (77 cm)	**H**
42	fig	*Ficus retusa*	30¼ in (77 cm)	**H**
43	Chinese ash	*Fraxinus chinensis*	21 in (53 cm)	**Pe**
44	manna ash	*Fraxinus ornus*	12½ in (32 cm)	**Fnz**
45	maidenhair tree	*Ginkgo biloba*	24½ in (62 cm)	**Pa**
46		*Holarrhena antidysenterica*	25 in (64 cm)	**H**
47	jacaranda	*Jacaranda mimosifolia*	22 in (56 cm)	**H**
48	winter jasmine	*Jasminum nudiflorum*	15 in (38 cm)	**PC**
49	needle juniper	*Juniperus rigida*	23½ in (60 cm)	**H**
50	Chinese juniper	*Juniperus sargentii*	20½ in (52 cm)	**Pe**
51	crape myrtle	*Lagerstroemia indica*	34½ in (88 cm)	**H**
52	European larch	*Larix decidua*	30 in (76 cm)	**Fg**
53	Japanese larch	*Larix kaempferi*	35½ in (90 cm)	**H**
54	glossy privet	*Ligustrum lucidum*	30¼ in (77 cm)	**Fmb**
55	Japanese privet	*Ligustrum sinense*	12¼ in (31 cm)	**Pe**
56	liquidambar	*Liquidambar formosana*	21 in (53 cm)	**Pe**
57	East Indian satin wood	*Maba buxifolia*	34¼ in (87 cm)	**Pe**
58	Hall's crab apple	*Malus halliana*	18 in (46 cm)	**H**
59	crab apple	*Malus pumila*	13¾ in (35 cm)	**H**
60		*Millettia japonica*	27 in (69 cm)	**H**

61	white mulberry	*Morus alba*	15¾ in (40 cm)	**Feb**
62	orange jasmine	*Murraya paniculata*	33 in (84 cm)	**Pe**
63	common myrtle	*Myrtus communis*	11¾ in (30 cm)	**Tms**
64	common olive	*Olea europaea*	35 in (89 cm)	**Pe**
65	wild olive	*Olea europaea* ssp. *oleaster*	20½ in (52 cm)	**Fg**
66	hop hornbeam	*Ostrya carpinifolia*	24½ in (62 cm)	**Tlv**
67		*Phillyrea angustifolia*	20½ in (52 cm)	**Ta**
68	Norway spruce	*Picea abies*	26¾ in (68 cm)	**Fg**
69	white spruce	*Picea glauca 'conica'*	29½ in (75 cm)	**Fg**
70	Yezo spruce	*Picea jezoensis*	36¼ in (92 cm)	**H**
71	arolla pine	*Pinus cembra*	26¾ in (68 cm)	**Fg**
72	Japanese red pine	*Pinus densiflora*	26¾ in (68 cm)	**H**
73	mountain pine	*Pinus mugo*	5½ in (14 cm)	**Fg**
74	black pine	*Pinus nigra*	22½ in (57 cm)	**Fg**
75	Japanese white pine	*Pinus parviflora*	37½ in (95 cm)	**H**
76	Scots pine	*Pinus sylvestris*	21¾ in (55 cm)	**Fmb**
77	Japanese black pine	*Pinus thunbergii*	9 in (23 cm)	**Fg**
78	Japanese brocade pine	*Pinus thunbergii* var. *'corticosa'*	35½ in (90 cm)	**PC**
79	Chinese pistachio	*Pistacia chinensis*	31½ in (80 cm)	**Pa**
80	mastic tree	*Pistacia lentiscus*	15¼ in (39 cm)	**Fmb**
81		*Pithecellobium dulce*	23½ in (60 cm)	**H**
82		*Podocarpus nagi*	33½ in (85 cm)	**Pe**
83	elephant bush	*Portulacaria afra*	19¼ in (49 cm)	**Pe**
84	potentilla	*Potentilla fruticosa*	11 in (28 cm)	**Pe**
85	apricot	*Prunus armeniaca*	15¾ in (40 cm)	**L**
86	Saint Lucie cherry	*Prunus mahaleb*	16 in (41 cm)	**Fg**
87	Japanese apricot	*Prunus mume*	27½ in (70 cm)	**PC**
88	peach	*Prunus persica*	15 in (38 cm)	**Pa**
89	flowering quince	*Pseudocydonia sinensis*	33½ in (85 cm)	**H**
90	golden larch	*Pseudolarix amabilis*	16½ in (42 cm)	**Fg**
91	pomegranate	*Punica granatum*	30¾ in (78 cm)	**Fg**
92	dwarf pomegranate	*Punica granatum* var. *'nana'*	8 in (20 cm)	**Pe**
93	firethorn	*Pyracantha coccinea*	35½ in (90 cm)	**H**
94	wild pear	*Pyrus pyraster*	10¼ in (26 cm)	**Ffb**
95	holly oak	*Quercus ilex*	31½ in (80 cm)	**Ta**
96	English oak	*Quercus robur*	35½ in (90 cm)	**Ta**
97	cork oak	*Quercus suber*	21¾ in (55 cm)	**Pi**
98	Setsuki azalea	*Rhododendron indicum*	17¾ in (45 cm)	**Fg**
99	smoke tree	*Rhus cotinus*	22 in (56 cm)	**Fmb**
100	gooseberry	*Ribes uva-crispa*	8 in (20 cm)	**Fmb**
101	rosemary	*Rosmarinus officinalis*	19¼ in (49 cm)	**Ffb**
102	theezan tea	*Sageretia thea*	22½ in (57 cm)	**H**
103	white willow	*Salix alba* var. *'tristis'*	24¾ in (63 cm)	**H**
104	Queensland umbrella tree	*Schefflera actinopylla*	19¾ in (50 cm)	**H**

105		*Scolopia chinensis*	22¾ in (58 cm)	**Pe**
106	Narihira bamboo	*Semiarundinaria fastuosa*	25½ in (65 cm)	**H**
107	big tree (dwarf)	*Sequoiadendron giganteum* var. 'pygmaeum'	34 in (86 cm)	**Fg**
108		*Serissa foetida*	26 in (66 cm)	**H**
109		*Spiraea japonica*	7 in (18 cm)	**H**
110	dwarf lilac	*Syringa microphylla*	14½ in (37 cm)	**Fg**
111	tamarind	*Tamarindus indica*	22½ in (57 cm)	**H**
112	tamarisk	*Tamarix chinensis*	34½ in (88 cm)	**Fg**
113	bald cypress	*Taxodium distichum*	31 in (79 cm)	**Fg**
114	English yew	*Taxus baccata*	28½ in (72 cm)	**H**
115	Japanese yew	*Taxus cuspidata*	13 in (33 cm)	**C**
116	thyme	*Thymus vulgaris*	9¾ in (25 cm)	**Pe**
117	littleleaf linden/lime	*Tilia cordata*	27½ in (70 cm)	**H**
118	eastern hemlock	*Tsuga canadensis* var. 'minima'	9½ in (24 cm)	**Fg**
119	Japanese hemlock	*Tsuga diversifolia*	30 in (76 cm)	**H**
120	Chinese elm	*Ulmus parvifolia*	38½ in (98 cm)	**H**
121		*Vitex negundo*	18½ in (47 cm)	**Pe**
122	Japanese wisteria	*Wisteria floribunda*	21¾ in (55 cm)	**H**
123	Caucasian elm	*Zelkova carpinifolia*	9 in (23 cm)	**H**
124	Zelkova	*Zelkova serrata*	25 in (64 cm)	**Pa**
p. 242	maidenhair tree	*Ginkgo biloba*	24½ in (62 cm)	**H**
p. 252	Japanese hornbeam	*Carpinus laxiflora*	27½ in (70 cm)	**Pa**

GLOSSARY

Achene Dry one-seeded fruit with tight, thin outer wall which does not open when ripe.

Acicular Needle-like.

Alkaloid Organic compound containing carbon, hydrogen, and nitrogen which has a basic reaction. Generally of plant origin, sometimes with therapeutic or toxic properties.

Alternate Arrangement of leaves which are placed at different heights on either side of the stem.

Aril Fleshy appendage of the funiculus which partially or wholly covers the seed.

Axil Upper angle formed by a leaf and its stalk on a stem.

Berry A pulpy or fleshy fruit with pericarp containing one or more hard-coated seeds.

Bilobate Divided into two lobes, as of a leaf.

Bipinnate Doubly pinnate, as of a leaf consisting of a central axis and lateral axes to which leaflets are attached.

Bisexual Plant bearing separate functional male and female flowers.

Bract Leaf-like appendage at base of a flower or enfolding an inflorescence, often brightly colored.

Calyx Outer ring of sepals beneath the petals, serving to protect the flower when in bud.

Catkin String of single-sex flowers, without petals, often pendulous.

Compound leaf A leaf, consisting of 2 or more leaflets.

Cone Fruit of a conifer consisting of woody scales enclosing naked multiple ovules or seeds.

Cordate Heart-shaped.

Coriaceous Having the texture or consistency of leather.

Corymb Flat or convex inflorescence with longer outer flower stalks.

Crenate Narrowly toothed, more or less rounded, as of a leaf margin.

Cultivar Cultivated variety.

Deciduous Referring to plants that drop their leaves at the end of a growing season.

Dentate Sharply toothed, as of leaf margins.

Digitate Finger-like, with radiating lobes or leaflets.

Dioecious Having male and female organs on separate plants.

Drupe A simple, fleshy fruit consisting of 3 layers: an outer skin, an inner fleshy portion, and a hard inner shell, usually enclosing one seed.

Endocarp   Inner protective layer of pericarp around seed.

Epicarp   Outer protective layer of pericarp.

Filiform   Thread-like.

Glabrous   Smooth, without hairs.

Gland   Small liquid-secreting structure or organ on or near surface of plant.

Glaucous   Gray–blue.

Glucoside   Plant or animal substance which together with other molecular aggregates contains a molecule of a sugar, decomposed by enzymes.

Hybrid   Plant created by crossing two species of the same genus or two varieties of the same species.

Imparipinnate   Of a leaf, pinnate with a terminal leaflet.

Indehiscent   Not opening at maturity.

Inflorescence   Flowering part of a plant, in form of an umbel, spike, raceme, spadix, cyme, corymb, catkin, etc.

Internode   Section of a stem between two successive nodes.

Involucre   Collection of bracts, usually around the base of a flower cluster.

Lanceolate   Lance-shaped.

Lateral   Positioned at side; extension of a branch or shoot.

Legume   Pod or seed vessel of the pea family, splitting lengthwise to release seeds.

Linear   Long and narrow, with parallel sides.

Lobe   Projection or division of a leaf or petal.

Membranous   Of thin, papery consistency.

Monoecious   Separate male and female flowers on the same plant.

Mucronate   Terminating in a point.

Node   Joint occurring at intervals along stem of a plant, from which a leaf or bud develops.

Oleoresin   Essential oil mixed with resin, secreted by certain plants.

Opposite   Leaf arrangement in pairs along an axis, one opposite the other.

Ovate   Egg-shaped, with larger part towards the base.

Palmate   With leaflets or lobes radiating like outstretched fingers from central point.

Panicle   Indeterminate, compound flower structure with groups of flowers on short stalks.

Papilionaceous   Referring to a corolla with separated petals arranged in the form of a butterfly.

Peduncle   Stalk of a flower or inflorescence.

Perennial   Plant that lives for three years or more.

Perianth   Envelope of a flower, including petals and sepals.

Pericarp   Wall of a ripened ovary or fruit, sometimes consisting of three layers, epicarp, mesocarp, and endocarp.

Petiole   Leaf stalk.

Pinnate   Compound leaf with leaflets, usually paired, on either side of the stalk.

Pistil   Female reproductive parts of flower, comprising ovary, style, and stigma.

Pneumatophore   A modified root which serves as a respiratory organ for many aquatic or bog plants.

Polymorphous   Of various forms or stages.

Pome   Fruit with fleshy body and cartilaginous core enclosing seeds, as apple, pear, quince, etc.

Prostrate   Habit of a plant with branches that creep along the ground.

Pubescent   Covered with short, soft hairs.

Raceme   Simple, unbranched inflorescence with flowers on an elongated axis.

Revolute   Rolled backwards, as of a leaf margin or petal.

Rhizome   Modified stem which develops horizontally underground.

Samara   Indehiscent dry winged fruit.

Sessile   Attached by base, without stalk.

Spike   Inflorescence consisting of elongated axis with stalkless flowers arranged at intervals.

Squamous   Covered with scales.

Stamen   Male part of flower, consisting of anther and filament.

Stomate   Minute pore in the epidermis of a leaf or stem through which gases are exchanged.

Strobilus   Cone-like reproductive structure with spore-bearing appendages or scales.

Suberose   Cork-like.

Subulate   Awl-shaped, tapering to a pointed apex.

Succulent   Plant with swollen, fleshy leaves and stems capable of storing water.

Tap-root   Descending main root giving off small lateral roots.

Terminal   At or close to tip.

Trifid   Of a leaf or petal, divided into three lobes.

BIBLIOGRAPHY

Adams, Peter, SUCCESSFUL BONSAI GROWING, Ward Lock, London, 1978.

Barton, Dan, THE BONSAI BOOK, Ebury Press, London, 1989.

Botero, Beatriz & Botero, Martha Olga, HAGAMOS BONSAI, Calí, Colombia, 1987.

Brockman, C. Frank, TREES OF NORTH AMERICA, Golden Press, New York, 1979.

Encke F., Buccheim G., Seibold S., ZANDER, HANDWÖRTERBUCH DER PFLANZENNAMEN, Eugen Ulmer, Stuggart, 1984.

Fenaroli L & Gambi G., ALBERI, Museo Tridentino di Scienze Naturali, Trento, 1976.

Gonzales, Gina Lopez, LA GUIDA DE INCAFO DE LOS ARBOLES Y AR-BUSTOS DE LA PENINSULA IBERICA, Incafo, Madrid, 1982.

Graf, Dr Alfred, EXOTICA INTERNATIONAL, VOL 1 & II, Roehers Company, U.S.A., 1986.

Hall, Doug & Black Don, THE SOUTH AMERICAN BONSAI BOOK, Howard Timmins, Capetown, 1979.

Hart, C., BRITISH TREES IN COLOUR, Michael Joseph, London, 1973.

Hilliers & Sons, HILLIERS MANUAL OF TREES & SHRUBS, David & Charles, London, 1981.

Hull, George F., BONSAI FOR AMERICANS, Doubleday & Co. Ltd., New York, 1964.

Katayama, Tei'ichi, THE MINI-BONSAI HOBBY, Japan Publications Inc., Tokyo, 1974.

Kawamoto, Toshio, SAIKEI: LIVING LANDSCAPE IN MINIATURE, Kodansha International, Tokyo, 1970.

Kawasumi, Masakuni, BONSAI WITH AMERICAN TREES, Kodansha International, Tokyo, 1975.

Kawasumi, Masakuni, INTRODUCTORY BONSAI, Ward Lock Ltd., London, 1971.

Kimball, Pipe Ann, BONSAI: THE ART OF DWARFING TREES, Hawthorn & Co. Inc., New York, 1964.

Koreshoff, Deborah R., BONSAI, Boolarong Publications, Brisbane, 1984.

La Rosa de Cuenca, Mercedes & Rauber Herrera, Milagros, EL BONSAI EN VENEZUELA, Caracas, 1984.

Lee Behme, Robert, BONSAI, SAIKEI AND BONKEI, W. Morrow & Co. Inc., New York, 1964.

Lesniewicz, Ilona & Zhimin, Li, PENJING, Hartmut Brückner, Bremen, 1987.

Lesniewicz, Paul, BONSAI MINIATURE BAÜME, Bonsai Centrum, Heidelberg, 1980.

Lesniewicz, Paul, INDOOR BONSAI, Blandford Press, Dorset, 1985.

Magrini, Gigliola, LE CONIFERE, Görlich, Milano, 1967.

Maumené, Albert, LES ARBRES NAINS JAPONAIS, Librairie Horticole, Paris, 1902.

Mitchell, Alain, A FIELD GUIDE TO THE TREES OF BRITAIN AND NORTHERN EUROPE, Collins, London, 1974.

Murata, Kenji, PRACTICAL BONSAI FOR BEGINNERS, Japan Publications Trading Co., Tokyo, 1969.

Naka, John Y., BONSAI TECHNIQUES I, Landman, Los Angeles, 1975.

Naka, John Y., BONSAI TECHNIQUES II, Landman, Los Angeles, 1982.

Nakamura, Zeko, BONSAI IN MINIATURA, Lib. Meravigli Ed., Vimercate, 1988.

Newsom, Samuel, A DWARFED TREE MANUAL FOR WESTERNERS, Tokyo News Service Ltd., Tokyo, 1964.

Notter, Pius, BONSAI, Basilius Verlag, Basel, 1987.

Ory, Pascal, LES EXPOSITIONS UNIVERSELLES DE PARIS, Ramsay, Paris, 1982.

Pareh, Jyoti, TROPICAL BONSAI, Vakils, Feffer & Simons Ltd, Bombay, 1977.

Pareh, Jyoti & Nikuny, WONDERLAND OF TROPICAL BONSAI, Valkils, Feffer & Simons Ltd., Bombay, 1987.

Perry Alstradt, Lynn, BONSAI: TREES AND SHRUBS, The Ronald Press Co., New York, 1964.

Perry Alstradt, Lynn & Young, Dorothy, BONSAI MANUAL, ABS, Erie, 1974.

Philips, Roger, TREES OF NORTH AMERICA AND EUROPE, Random House, New York, 1978.

Ricchiari, Antonio, MANUALE DEL BONSAI, Lib. Dario Flaccovio Ed., Palermo, 1987.

Stowell, Jerald P., THE BEGINNER'S GUIDE TO AMERICAN BONSAI, Kodansha International Ltd., Tokyo, 1978.

Valevanis, William N., JAPANESE FIVE-NEEDLE PINE, Symmes Systems, Atlanta, 1976.

Walker, Linda M., BONSAI, J. Gifford Ltd., London, 1978.

Yashiroda, Kan, BONSAI, Faber and Faber, London, 1960.

Yoshimura, Yuji & Halford, Giovanna M., THE JAPANESE ART OF MINIATURE TREES AND LANDSCAPES, Charles E. Tuttle Co., Rutland, 1957.

Young, Dorothy S., BONSAI – THE ART AND TECHNIQUE, Prentice-Hall, New Jersey, 1985.

INDEX